WINTER WONDER

WRITINGS FROM OUR NECK OF THE WOODS

VICTORIA COLVER * CLARK GRAHAM *
DEB GRAHAM * L.P. MASTERS * SHANNA
L.K. MILLER * TYLER POWELL * ALLI RIGGS
* KATHRYN ROSENBAUM * KIM ROTH

CONTENTS

1. Who Makes the Best Cookies in the World, Santa?   7
   By Tyler Powell

2. Snapshot   11
   By Shanna L. K. Miller

3. Unholy Friends   15
   By Clark Graham

4. A Reaper Christmas   19
   By Alli Riggs

5. A Christmas Tale of Gifts, Santa Claus, and Grace   45
   By Kim Roth

6. Seasons Grieving   79
   By Shanna L. K. Miller

7. Doorbell Ditching with Olly T   83
   By Kathryn Rosenbaum

8. Holiday Greetings   129
   By Shanna L. K. Miller

9. An Untraditional Christmas   135
    By Clark Graham

10. A Smuggled Christmas: A Venusian Skies Short Story   143
    By L.P. Masters

11. Firehouse Christmas Party   157
    By Deb Graham

12. Grandma's Glorious Gifts   185
    By Shanna L. K. Miller

13. Hard to Save   189
    By L.P. Masters

14. Home for Christmas   203
    By Victoria Colver
        Part 1: Clive
        Christmas, 1934
        Part 2: Dorothy
        Christmas, WWII
        Part 3: Julianne
        Christmas, 2024

15. Author Biographies   251
    Victoria Colver
    Clark Graham
    Deb Graham
    L.P. Masters
    Shanna L. K. Miller
    Tyler Scott Powell
    Alli Riggs
    Kathryn Rosenbaum

Kim Roth

WHO MAKES THE BEST COOKIES IN THE WORLD, SANTA?

BY TYLER POWELL

My boys sat on Santa's lap earlier today. To my surprise, they didn't come prepared with a wishlist—they came with questions.

"What is your favorite food?"

"Why, cookies of course! Your mother nailed it last year—not all cookies are created equal, let me tell you!"

"Were they the best cookies you've ever had?"

"Well boys, you have to remember I've been doing this for hundreds of years. When you've eaten as many cookies as I have—about a trillion—the competition gets pretty stiff, I have to be honest. They were ten-out-of-ten though, no question about that. Best in all of North America."

"Who makes the best cookies in the world?"

"That would be Mrs. Claus! Her cookies almost bring a tear to my eye, every time, and she makes cookies quite often at the North Pole!"

"What does she do that makes her cookies so good? Is there a river of chocolate in the North Pole that makes the most delicious chocolate chips? Do the elves help her make homemade peanut butter?"

"Chocolate rivers do make delicious chocolate chips, and the elves can make a good peanut butter, but those aren't the reasons her cookies are the best!"

"Does the North Pole have the happiest cows that make the most delicious milk? Do the happiest chickens lay the best eggs?"

"Every animal in the North Pole is very happy; the elves take great care of them. But that's not it either."

"Does Mrs. Claus always get her recipe perfect? Is she the most-master cookie-chef ever?"

"Hundreds of years of trial and error will get you a perfect recipe, and she never errs anymore, but even that isn't the reason her cookies are the best in the world."

"Then what *is* the reason?"

"Well boys, let me tell you a story..."

"Once upon a time, when my hair was red instead of white, and I weighed about a hundred pounds less, I was having a very bad day. Even Santa Claus has bad days sometimes, and Young Kris Kringle had a lot of bad days in the beginning. Working out the logistics behind coordinating an army of elves to make toys for every good girl and boy over the whole world was a nightmare. There were challenges from start to finish, and honestly new challenges still come up now and again. Before I figured out how to use my magic, and before the elves became masters of the craft of the toy-making we know today, we were hitting snags left and right. The elves caught on quickly to carving tops and spinners, whirlers and wheels, they moved on to Jack-in-the-boxes, and music boxes, but technology progressed so quickly, and elves used to be real old-school. When toys moved away from woodwork, I started to worry we wouldn't be able to keep up. After a particularly rough training, I went for a walk and sat down, wanting to cry at the thought of all the good kids that had put faith in me to deliver their favorite presents on Christmas. I thought for sure we wouldn't be able to do it.

Well, Mrs. Claus knew my favorite treat. But she hated making cookies! She wasn't well-practiced, and burned them often. So she'd given up! She said I get enough treats to last me the year on Christmas, I don't need cookies. Which is true. And as I was sitting there so sad, I thought, *A cookie would be really nice right now*, and you'd never guess what happened! A plate of cookies fell in my lap! Mrs. Claus came to save the day.

That was the best plate of cookies I ever had in my life, not because Mrs. Claus suddenly became the best cookie maker overnight, but because I knew how much love she put into each one. She did it just for me.

It's hard to believe, but sometimes even at the North Pole, there are struggles and new challenges that arise, and even Santa Claus wonders, 'How will I make it through? This time might be the time it all falls apart.'

You boys are young now, but it may even happen to you one day when you have kids of your own that are depending on you. On days like that, the most valuable thing in the world you could have is a wife who will make you a plate of cookies, and let you know that she has confidence in you, even when you don't have confidence in yourself. How can you lose then?"

Kris Kringle would never have become Santa without Mrs. Claus.

SNAPSHOT

BY SHANNA L. K. MILLER

Snapshot

Grainy
Tone on tone
Preserved images

Contrast sharply against
Glossy deckled edge boundary.

Aging piece of time eagerly scanned.
Recollection searches for evidence beyond

Context of season, objects, furnishings, participants;
Attempts to fill in the blanks beyond snapshot's confines.

Recall no longer an absolute. Memory
Does not place captured moment, delighted smile,

Overalls, checked shirt. What colors were the checks? No matter.
Love and joy were there; are remembered. I tightly grasp their surety,

Hold them close.
Smile echoes smile.

Shanna L. K. Miller

UNHOLY FRIENDS

BY CLARK GRAHAM

As Susan opened the door, Linda walked in and handed her a casserole dish.

"Oh, your cheesy potatoes," Susan smiled. "I'll just set them on the dining room table. Dinner is almost ready so go sit for a minute."

"Can I help with anything?" Linda asked.

"Nope, just finishing up."

Christmas songs played softly in the background as Linda walked over and admired the Christmas tree with its red and white blinking lights and mismatched ornaments. She sat down on the couch by a preoccupied Dave. "Why aren't you in there helping your wife, little brother?"

"I've been banished."

"Banished? What did you do now?"

"Too much sampling. You would think she'd appreciate the opinion of an experienced taste tester, but no, she kicked me out." He went back to his phone.

Linda giggled. "I see. Who are you texting; anyone I know?"

"Oh, um, messaging, actually. Erik Jones."

"Erik Jones? Oh, wait, not Grumpy Old Man Jones who lived on the corner and used to swear at us for cutting across his lawn?"

Dave confirmed, "Yep, that's him."

"Why on earth are you friends with him?"

"He sent me a friend request and I thought, 'Oh, why not?'"

"You don't have to friend everyone who sends you a request, you know."

Dave hit send then set down his phone. "Mr. Jones would get home from his factory job and sit there on the porch until his wife would get home. After you headed off to college, I decided that I wanted to see that grumpy old man smile, so I made it my challenge to make that happen. One day I stopped in front of his house on my way home from school and told him a corny joke."

She shook her head. "How did that go over?"

"Not so good the first three days, but on the fourth day, he cracked a smile. On the ninth day, he laughed out loud. After I told a joke three weeks in, I turned to leave and he said, 'Stop, I have one too.' We exchanged jokes the rest of the school year. Did you know he's a member of the Church?"

"By his limited vocabulary the times I encountered him, I would not have guessed that."

"Yes, when the factory shut down, he and his wife were having a tough time of it. Dad was the bishop at the time and he called them up and asked them if they needed anything. They told him no. He knew better so he went to their house to check on them. They had no food. He had me help him deliver a grocery order to them. His wife burst into tears. He had tears brimming from his eyes too. They hugged us both before we left. I found out later, Dad even helped them with a house payment or two."

"Wow," Linda said.

"He found a job that required him to relocate. He began attending Church in his new ward. He's since retired and now works in the temple. We still send corny jokes back and forth by messaging each other."

A little girl with pigtails came into the room. "Mommy says supper is ready."

Dave stood and looked down at his sister on her phone. "What are you doing?"

Looking up Linda smiled. "Sending him a friend request. I like corny jokes, too."

A REAPER CHRISTMAS

BY ALLI RIGGS

Chapter 1: Clandestine Meetings

How can anyone be happy on Christmas when death surrounds them?

I stand at the top of Tower Mountain overlooking the city of Spokane, Washington. Admittedly, the city looks beautiful and serene, blanketed in snow, enveloped by mountains and pine trees. Lights twinkle from the cars and buildings below, even more than usual because of the season. Snowflakes flutter from the sky, kissing my nose and cheeks, silencing any wildlife in the forest surrounding me.

I close my eyes and breathe in the cool, crisp calm, centering myself and preparing for this evening's assignments. Never in my wildest dreams did I think I'd be a sixteen-year-old Grim Reaper. Or ever.

"Tim, I thought I'd find you here," Skye says from behind me. "This seems to be your favorite spot nowadays."

Her voice cocoons me like a downy quilt, making a slow smile spread across my face when I turn to her.

The white hood of Skye's Angel of Mercy robe covers her platinum hair, and the robe's hem skims the ground as she approaches, leaving a smooth pattern on the snow behind her.

She stops short of touching me and frowns. "You're not dressed to reap yet. Is something wrong?"

Shaking my head, I grab her hand and pull her closer. "I was about to leave. I'm having a hard time mustering the mood to work. It's Christmas and I keep thinking about how everyone who dies tonight will leave their family on Christmas. It'll ruin all future Christmases for their family and rip the dead from their loved ones on what's supposed to be a joyous occasion."

Skye nods slowly, her brows furrowed, and lips pressed thin. "Mother says the adversary works especially hard this time of year to create more misery to offset the joy. It's busier now for people like AOMs and Reapers than any day of the year because we're the ones who deal with grief, pain, and dying."

"Great," I mutter. "Because I don't have enough dead people to usher to the other side."

Skye rubs the back of my hand with her thumb. "She also says that the reception the departed receive in heaven is a sight to behold. It's *Christmas*. Haven't you ever wondered what heaven is like at Christmas?"

I gaze into Skye's ice-blue eyes, and they dance with excitement as she continues. "Mother says if we have a free moment, she'll let me see what it's like. You should ask your dad if he'll do the same for you."

She offers a wistful smile. "Mother says whatever a person loses by exiting this life during the holidays, they gain a hundredfold when they cross over. She's never seen an unhappy crossing."

"Never?" I ask, hope blooming in my gut.

Skye shakes her head. "Never. I wish the families left behind could understand what's waiting beyond."

In the pockets of my jeans, my multi-tool that houses my scythe vibrates. My stomach bottoms out and I groan before pressing my hand against the pocket. "Dad is calling me."

Skye turns and looks up at me, then smiles and gives me a quick peck on the cheek. She smells of flowers—peonies, I think. She told me once when I asked. Said they remind her of her grandmother. Skye bites her lip, pulling away, and glancing around, as if worried the Godfather himself will appear out of nothingness and reprimand us for touching. Though I wouldn't put it past him after one of the Four Horsemen visited us when we kissed for the first time.

My pocket vibrates again. This time my scythe radiates blistering heat. I hiss in pain.

Sky wrinkles her nose and straightens, pulling the warmth of her long, slender fingers from mine. "Your dad again?"

"I've got to go," I say.

Then quickly, before she can react, I give Skye a peck on the lips. It may have lasted only a millisecond, but her touch seers its memory onto my lips. Who knows how long I'll have to wait until I touch her again? With my luck, we'd set off the apocalypse or something.

Sky presses her fingers to her mouth and blinks several times before relaxing and bursting into a grin. "Merry Christmas, Tim. See you tomorrow at school?"

I nod. "Should we meet at *your* favorite place tomorrow night?"

A slow smile spreads across her lips, drawing my attention to them again. The familiar longing pools in my stomach, and I swallow. Family. We're *family* now. Nothing more.

"Sounds like a plan," she says. "It's much warmer in Fiji, anyway."

Before I can respond, she disappears into a wisp of glittery white smoke and mist.

My scythe vibrates again, and I roll my eyes, muttering, "I'm on my way."

Then I dematerialize into a wisp of red smoke, ready to reap.

Chapter 2: Reluctant Apprentice

When I meet my dad in the space I've dubbed the Death Depot, I've already changed into my black dress pants, a black button-down shirt, and matching dress shoes. I look identical to Dad, except even though he is more than eight hundred and fifty years older than I am, he only looks thirty-five.

Two months ago, when he told me he was a Grim Reaper and that I was to become his apprentice, I was five foot two, a hundred pounds sopping wet, and looked like a prepubescent boy.

Since I started reaping, I've grown fourteen inches and added over a hundred and fifty pounds in muscle mass. I look more like a professional athlete now, drawing the attention of both football and basketball coaches, and more than a few curious high school students.

Dad looks up from his massive wooden desk where he's sifting through a stack of parchment papers so tall he needs to stand to reach the top page. The papers constantly sway from side to side, on the verge of collapse, but never quite toppling.

I can't remember how many times I've sat and watched those papers, waiting for them to scatter all over his desk and onto the smooth cavern walls of the Death Depot.

"Where have you been?" Dad says, frowning. "We were supposed to start reaping thirty minutes ago."

"Procrastinating," I say, dropping into the musty velvet tufted chair in front of his desk and watching the dust explode from the seat.

He glances at a piece of paper before putting it in a file marked 'COMPLETE'. The paper disappears into thin air. "Why?"

"You know why." I scrub my hands down my face and groan, leaning back into the seat. "It's Christmas time. I hate taking people from their families this time of year. Can't we just *not* reap on Christmas?"

Dad pulls in a long-suffering breath. "We've been over this, Tim. This is your first Christmas. You're sixteen. You don't have the life experience—the *reaping* experience—to know what the nuances of this job are yet. Have faith. The holidays don't affect only people on Earth, they affect people in the afterlife too. You'll understand soon enough."

Resisting the urge to roll my eyes, I stand. "Let's get this night over with."

He nods and slides a piece of parchment paper to me. "Molly Stone is our first assignment. We have a full load tonight, so be sure to center yourself often to maintain your energy and power. The holidays are always busier than usual."

"Why?" I ask, taking the paper from him.

"The angels are celebrating. The demons are fuming that the angels are celebrating, so the demons take it out on the mortals."

"That sucks."

"Agreed."

I skim over the information on the paper, and my stomach twists tighter with each sentence until I finally look up at Dad, throwing my arms out in frustration. "You've got to be kidding me. We're taking a toddler tonight?"

Dad stands and puts his arm around my shoulder. "Yes. And Molly is going to be excited when she sees us."

"Why?" I glance down at the paper I'd skimmed over.

CAUSE OF DEATH: Organ failure

HISTORY: Childhood Leukemia

Something in my chest throbs and I rub at my heart to ease the pain. Tears spring to my eyes and I try to blink them away. "She's suffering here, isn't she?"

Dad nods. "Let's go take this little girl's suffering away."

I sniff and wipe at my cheeks, pull out my multi-tool knife and choose the scythe, enabling it to animate to full size. Then I follow Dad to our destination.

Going from the silence of the Death Depot to the utter chaos of the hospital room makes me flinch. When I get my bearings, I glance around, half-expecting emergency room personnel or nurses working frantically to save the girl.

But when I focus on the shoulder-to-shoulder spirits in the room, my eyes widen.

The hospital room is about eight feet by ten feet in size. It's a tiny space that smells of antiseptic with enough room for a hospital bed and two chairs. If you removed the hoard of spirits, I suspect the mortal's room would be absolutely silent, except for the beep of the monitors near the head of the girl's bed. She's a tiny girl with overly-chubby cheeks and a bald head with a tube sticking out of her arm and one out of her chest. Dark lashes flutter against her cheeks and a grimace forms on her mouth.

Her mother, a brunette with her hair pulled back into a low ponytail, and a red, splotchy face, holds her daughter's hand. The dad, a redhead with a matching goatee and hair sticking in all directions, has one hand pressed on his wife's back, and the other on his daughter's shoulder. His eyes are red-rimmed and his lips tremble with each breath.

My dad stands on the other side of the bed from me, next to the couple. He nods to the dozens of translucent bodies standing shoulder-to-shoulder, some of them seeming to overlap one another or partially inside one another so that they all can fit in the room. But none of them acknowledges me or Dad.

"What's going on?" I ask Dad in a low murmur. "Why are all these spirits here? Are they from the hospital?"

Dad shakes his head and grins. "This is the extended family that passed before Molly. They're here to witness her death."

"Can they see us?" I ask.

Dad shakes his head. "And Molly won't see them when she initially passes. But she will feel the love and excitement. Watch."

Almost as if on cue, the beeping on Molly's heart monitor stops, causing the machine to alarm.

Her mom's head jerks up, and she glances at the monitor. Tears drip down her cheeks, and a shuddered sob fills the room. I vaguely see a nurse scurry to the bedside, passing through Dad to get to the monitors, but it's overshadowed by the cheers of the spirits. They're deafening; Like everyone just watched the ball drop on New Year's Eve. They're hugging and celebrating Molly's death. Excitement rolls off them like heat waves in the desert.

Dad is already reaching out to Molly, pulling her spirit out of its body. His expression is warm and tender as she stands on her bed and reaches her arms out to him.

Unlike the tired, frail body in the hospital bed, this little girl has long red hair that falls in ringlets down her back, an energy that seems to hum, and strong arms that wrap around Dad's neck in a giant hug.

"Am I dead?" the tiny little voice says to him. She glances around and seems to notice me for the first time. "Are you dead too?"

I grin at the girl and shake my head then gesture to my dad. "I'm his apprentice. You're my first child."

Molly turns and looks Dad in the eyes, as if waiting for him to answer her initial question.

"Yes, honey. You are." Dad wraps his arms around her in a hug. "I'm here to take you to Heaven. There are so many people waiting there to see you." Dad lifts his head and looks around. "Can you feel how excited they are?"

A grin engulfs her face and she nods. "It feels like a great big hug."

Molly's mother lets out another sob and her dad hugs her, dropping his head to her shoulder.

Molly turns, her brows furrowed, and lips turned down. "They're sad."

"They miss you already," Dad says. "It'll be a long time until they get to see you again."

Molly's big brown eyes look up at Dad, shining with tears. "Can I stay?"

"I'd have to put you back in your body and you'd be sick again."

Molly frowns again.

"Tell you what," Dad says, still holding her in his arms. "How about you give each of them one more hug before you leave and I will make sure they feel you. Would that help?"

"How long will I be gone?" she asks, eying her sickly body on the hospital bed.

"A long time," Dad says. "But you can check on them any time you want in Heaven." A sly smile crosses his face. "Plus, we have a surprise for you. A special someone who can't wait to see you."

Molly's eyes brighten and she bounces on her toes in anticipation. "Really?"

Dad nods then gestures to her parents. "But first your parents."

Molly's frown reappears and she nods. Dad walks her over to her parents, and Molly leans down, wrapping her tiny arms around her mother's neck and pulling her into a hug.

"I love you," Molly whispers into her mother's ear, then kisses her hair. She does the same with her father. Each parent calms, their tears slowing to shuddered breaths.

When Dad straightens again, Molly turns to him. "Will they be okay?"

"It will take a while. They love you so much," Dad says. "But they will be okay. And when they see you again, you can throw the biggest party and invite all your friends."

Molly's eyes light up again. "Really?"

"Yep! Wait till you get to Heaven. It's so much better there. And, since you're going to Heaven on Christmas, you get an extra surprise." Dad grins at her, then his gaze meets mine.

"Meet you there?" he says.

I catch Molly's eye and say, "I'll race you!" Then I disappear into a puff of red smoke.

Chapter 3: Family Reunions

The second I rematerialize in Processing, I jerk and look around. Everything has changed since yesterday.

Yesterday, a long row of angels sat behind mist-drenched desks processing the deceased. A white ethereal glow filled the room from all sides, infusing warmth and happiness into the atmosphere. Like every other day, Reapers popped in and out of existence with their people, bringing them to the angels to be processed.

But today? Whoa.

Twinkling lights cover everything as if we're standing on a cloud that's drifted into a massive cluster of stars. The atmosphere is warm and soothing; A combination of smells I can't pick apart, but when I inhale, it reminds me of coming home. Wrapped in a hug, kisses good night, and whispered I love you's all woven into a scent that instantly tells my soul that I'm safe here.

Even the atmosphere feels different. Excited. Giddy. There's some sort of pulsing in the air, but not like the beat of a bass blasting from a speaker. More like a...a...I can't put my finger on it.

Dad appears in front of me, giggling with Molly still in his arms. She's making funny faces at him, and playing with his hair, pulling it up to make horns or something.

As soon as they appear, she drops his hair, and her eyes bulge, her tiny mouth forming a giant O. She slides out of Dad's arms and onto the clouds. Her bare feet seem to sink into the clouds until the wisps of white mist cover the tops of her wiggling toes. With a reverential whisper, she twirls around and says, "What is this place?"

Dad squats next to her, still grinning. "It's Heaven, honey. "It's your reward for putting up with so much while you were alive. Now you spend eternity up here. No pain. No sadness. No struggle." He jerks his head toward the bank of angels. "Let's get you checked in."

Dad grabs Molly's little hand and walks her up to the processing desks. There's one angel on the end whose desk sits much lower than the others. When I first started reaping, I thought it was for wheelchairs, then I did a facepalm. Nobody has a wheelchair after they die. That's a mortality thing. The short desk is for children.

When Dad and Molly reach the short desk, they encounter a matronly-looking woman with amber-colored eyes. Her long white hair seems to skim the clouds at her feet. Wrinkles etch her cheeks and jowls, and round-rimmed glasses perch on her button nose.

The woman inclines her head toward the little girl. "Well, hello, my dear. What is your name?"

"Molly," the little girl says as she holds the hem of her Disney Princess nightgown, twirling it from side to side.

"Very nice to meet you, Molly, dear. My name is Eve. We're so excited you're here. Everyone's been abuzz about your arrival. They're waiting for you on the other side of that door."

The angel points to a golden door off to the side, and then she says to Dad, "If you will do the honors, Edgar."

Molly's gaze fixates on the door, and she grips Dad's hand. "Is this my surprise?"

Dad nods. "Someone very special to you is waiting for you on the other side, along with a whole bunch of others."

Molly's eyes widen. "I can hear them!" She surges forward like a kid trying to get into a candy store.

Dad practically stumbles behind her, trying to keep up. When she gets to the door, Molly reaches for the knob and yanks it open. Music erupts from the other side, hitting me in a wave, and making me stumble backward a couple of steps. It's like standing in front of a ten-foot-high speaker emitting Christmas music. Except this isn't something from a music track. It's concourses of angels—honest-to-goodness angels singing and rejoicing.

Every other day you'd hear a low hum of music, kind of like an afterthought. But today, I feel like my eardrum might burst from the decibel levels, and I'll go blind from the light shining through the door.

Chills crawl up my arms and down my neck as the sound washes over and through me. I listen to the words, the celebration, and the sheer *joy*. When I open my eyes, any angst I'd had about today is gone. Not only gone, but I'm questioning why I even worried in the first place.

I glance over at Eve. She's giving me a knowing grin. "First time?" she asks.

I nod.

"I volunteer to man the desks every Christmas," she says, a twinkle in her eye. "I love to watch everyone experience Heaven on this day. It's not like anything else in all of eternity."

I cough out a chuckled agreement. "It sure beats going to Disneyland."

Eve laughs. "Nothing on Earth compares to Heaven." She slides a look over to the door where Molly has already disappeared and Dad is standing at the threshold talking to someone.

"You wanna peek inside?" Eve asks.

My eyes widen and an excitement akin to an eight-year-old opening a massive present at Christmas blossoms inside my chest. "Can I?"

"Just this once," she says. "As long as you don't step over the threshold. Stay on this side and you'll be fine." She gives me a wink, then shoos me with her hands. "Hurry before someone catches us!"

I scurry to the doorway and stop next to Dad. He glances back at me before putting his arm around my shoulder, pulling me close, and murmuring, "This is why Christmas is the best time to die."

I stare at the expanse in front of me, my mouth gaping, and probably looking like a complete and utter fool. But I can't help it. Words don't describe what I see. And yet, I'll never forget it. Not till the day I die...*if* I ever die.

The space where the sky should be has a cream hue that glows, like a gossamer curtain covering the sun. The stars pulse to the music, and the choir of angels seems to go on forever, well beyond my sight. Their wings frame the choir like a feathery backdrop, fluttering in a breeze that smells of honeysuckle and fresh-cut grass.

Heaven stretches forever, with rolling hills, snow-covered mountains, winding streams, waterfalls of varying heights and widths, and trees as far as the eye can see. Meandering pathways gilded in gold bisect the lush grass and fragrant meadows. Animals of every shape and size mingle with humans and each other. There's literally a lion lying down with a lamb nestled between his legs, the lamb's head resting on the lion's paws.

Molly is surrounded by hundreds upon hundreds of cheering people. A man about Dad's age lifts her onto his shoulders and twirls around for everyone to see her grinning face.

"Who is she with?" I ask Dad, nodding toward Molly.

"That's her grandfather. He died of a heart attack the week before her. He used to visit her every day in the hospital and cared for Molly while her parents worked and cared for her siblings." Dad points to the others surrounding Molly. "Those are relatives and loved ones who passed before her. Some of them were in her hospital room when she passed. They're here to celebrate her return to Heaven and watch over her until the rest of her family gets here."

"This place is nothing like I pictured it," I say.

Dad chuckles and rubs his neck. "Yeah. Nobody gets it right. Everyone seems to have a snippet correct, but how do you describe a place like this? The way it makes you feel? How everyone seems to know and love everyone else? How money and fame no longer matter, only love and kindness?"

He gestures to the lion and the lamb. "Even the animals are here, but the malice is gone. Protectors in life *and* death. And if a person ever had a family pet, the pet is here waiting for them." He leans into me and murmurs, "Those reunions are cool to–"

A stunning woman materializes in front of me and Dad in an explosion of white smoke. Her wavy brown hair and green eyes are identical to mine, and the top of her head reaches my shoulder.

Dad's eyes widen and he steps away from her, dropping his arms from around my shoulders. "Melissa."

The woman doesn't even acknowledge my dad, which, to be honest, never happens because as far as guys go, he's pretty stinking handsome—or so I'm told. He's got broad, muscular shoulders like mine, black hair, straight white teeth, and piercing green eyes. I've never *not* seen women (and a few teenage girls) hit on him. It's disgusting, to be honest. But Dad ignores most of it.

Here and now, this woman doesn't acknowledge Dad's existence. Her focus is entirely on me. It takes half a second for me to recognize her. Probably because she doesn't quite look like her photos. She's a little younger, and the photos don't do her looks any justice.

But when it clicks, my lips start to tremble and my eyes fill with tears.

"Mom?" I croak, my mouth opening and closing like a fish trying to get water.

"Timmy." The woman pulls me into a fierce hug, silently sobbing into my shoulder. "You're all grown up."

When she pulls away, she drags her hand through her long brown hair, shakes her head, and pulls me into another stunned hug.

I stare at Dad. He stares at me, his face mirroring what mine must look like.

I wrap my arms around her and squeeze. Taking in the reality that for the first time in my sixteen years of existence, I'm talking to—holding—my mom. The woman who died while giving birth to me.

I press my eyes closed, letting my tears fall, and then squeeze harder. I never want to let this woman go. "Mom."

When she finally pulls away, she laughs and drags her hand through her hair again. "I guess it's a good thing we don't cry in heaven. I'd be a complete mess."

I wipe my eyes and nod. "Yeah. Who wants to see that?"

Mom chuckles, shaking her head. "You've turned into a man."

Finally, she looks over my shoulder at my dad, her demeanor cooling. "And you haven't changed a bit."

"H-hello, Melissa."

As if dismissing him, she turns back to me, grabbing my hands. "How are you doing? How's life? Has Edgar taken care of you? Are you happy? Do you have a girlfriend?"

"Whoa. Whoa. Whoa!" I hold up both hands in surrender.

Mom pulls me into another hug. "Sorry. I have so many questions and so little time." She glances over my shoulder into the processing room where Dad and I are standing.

I glance over my shoulder, following Mom's gaze and catch Eve's eyes. She winks at me and waves her hand. "You still have a few minutes."

Mom ducks her head, looking at me again and repeats, "Are you happy? Is your dad taking good care of you?"

Dad and I lock eyes. He looks pale like the world will crumble around us if I say the wrong thing. So I smile at him before focusing on Mom and saying, "Yeah. I'm happy. It hasn't been easy without you. I miss you—we both do. But we manage. And Dad takes good care of me."

Mom nods and glances over at Dad again before asking, "Any girl-friends?"

Only the one that'd probably start an apocalypse if I dated. "Nope."

She smooths her hand down my arm. "You've got plenty of time. Hundreds of years, apparently." She chuckles then lets out a sigh and turns, focusing on Dad. "Edgar."

Dad swallows again. "Melissa."

Is that all the man can say right now? Sheesh. No wonder he doesn't date women. The guy's got no skills. He'd be wringing his hat right now if he had one.

Mom sighs and dips her chin, looking up at him through her lashes. "I guess I deserve that. The last time we spoke was...emotional."

Dad clears his throat. "Yeah."

Mom sighs again. Is she a sigher? I guess she's a sigher. Dad never mentioned that about her.

"So, I've met all your other wives," she says, making her eyes go wide for emphasis.

"And?" Dad croaks.

"And they all seem pretty nice. Aside from the dark hair and being utterly *gorgeous*, they all seem to have one thing in common that I don't have."

"What?" I ask.

"All of his other wives have been married before they married your dad," she says, turning to me. "But your dad was my first marriage."

Mom tilts her head at Dad and narrows her eyes. "Why is that? All those other women have a husband, even a few children from the first marriage they get to spend eternity with up here. But I have nothing. You and Tim will live forever, and I'll be here flitting around tagging along with other families like a third wheel."

Mom's face cracks and her lips tremble. "Why would you do that to me?"

Dad tries to pull her into a hug, but she shrugs him off, turning her back to both of us. Her voice is hard and angry when she asks, "Why didn't you tell me the truth and let me make the decision myself, Edgar?"

Dad winces like each word is a punch to the face. He scratches his temple and presses his eyes closed. "Because I wanted you all to myself. The plan was to have Tim, raise him, train him, and then return to you once I knew he was established in his own life."

He starts to step closer to Mom, but Eve hollers, "Do NOT cross that threshold!"

Dad cringes and puts his foot firmly on the proper side of the door. "Time passes faster here than it does on Earth. It's been sixteen long, miserable years without you," he says. "How long has it been for you without me?"

Mom turns slightly, staring at her hands. "A couple of days."

"You're still fuming from everything that just happened," Dad says. "I've wallowed in misery for years, kicking myself for all the wrongs I did, wishing I could go back and fix them."

Dad grabs my shoulder, squeezing it. "But if I return to you, that means I'm leaving Tim, and you'd never take me back if I did that. I have to finish what I started. And I have to do it right. But I promise you that if you'll have me, I *will* be back. And we *will* be together forever."

A sob escapes Mom's lips and she turns, stepping into Dad's arms, and pressing her face into his chest, hugging him. He rubs his hand up and down her back, tears streaming down his face. He kisses the top of her head. "I'm so sorry."

When Mom finally pulls away, she looks up at Dad and smooths a lock of his dark hair out of his eyes. "I've also heard you haven't re-married since me."

Dad snorts and wipes at his eyes. "Nobody can replace you, my love."

"You'd better believe it." She narrows her eyes at him. "And you'd better keep it that way."

"Yes, dear."

Mom pulls Dad into one more hug and says, "Death was worth it to get Timmy."

Then she drags me into another hug. "I love you, Tim. Never forget that. Death was worth every second of pain, every moment of missing you, and every ounce of sadness I've felt since we parted to have you. I'm always watching you, even when you can't see me. And I will never stop loving you."

Crap! Now she's got me crying again too.

All those years I wondered about who my mom was, what she was like, how she would feel about me, and what we would have been like as a family. She consumed my thoughts and my heart.

Now, I can't help it. I'm freaking sobbing like a baby.

Mom smooths her hands over my head and holds me, rocking from side to side. "Shh. Shh. It's going to be all right. It's all for the best. All of this makes you a better man. And a more compassionate reaper." She pulls away from me, offering a sad smile. "And you truly are an amazing young man."

Mom glances over at Dad. "You were raised well. Just don't tell *him* that. Let's make him suffer a little longer." She winks and gives a knowing smile.

Dad rolls his eyes and grins.

"It's time to go!" Eve calls from her chair. "Fifteen seconds."

Dad nods at Eve.

Mom pulls me into one more desperate hug, then steps away, back into Heaven. She smooths her long white dress and wrings her hands. "Edgar, when you decide that the time is right, I'll be waiting for you."

Dad opens his mouth to say something, but the door slams shut, leaving us standing there staring at its ornate carvings, stunned into silence.

"Psst!" Eve whisper-yells. "Get outta here. Someone's coming."

Chapter 4: Christmas Wishes

Thank goodness Dad knows how to slow time to get all our work done in one night because I'm pretty sure we completed a week's worth of work in one mortal hour.

Yet, every time we return to Processing with another person, watching them experience Heaven at Christmas invigorates me. I don't need to recenter and recharge my energy a single time the entire night.

When Dad and I finally arrive at our home in the mortuary, I'm bouncing off the walls like a ten-year-old who stole five pounds of candy and gobbled it in one sitting.

Dad chuckles and shakes his head. "Why don't you get our gifts and I'll grab some food? I'll meet you at the Christmas tree in fifteen minutes."

"I'm on it," I holler over my shoulder, already halfway down the hall to my room.

Christmas is a low-key affair at our house. It always has been. Now that I know what Dad does in his spare time, I understand why.

I grab my customary three gifts from under my bed.

A few minutes later, Dad walks in with frozen pizzas cooked, cut, and arranged on two dinner plates. "Voilà! Dinner o' champions!"

I rub my hands together and inhale the garlic and tomato scent. My watering mouth wars with my grumbling stomach to decide which one is more insistent.

Dad chuckles and pulls a bottle of Dr. Pepper from the pocket of his pants, handing it to me before producing another one from his other pocket.

He sinks into the overstuffed recliner adjacent to the sofa and opens the soda, letting it hiss as the pressure discharges from the bottle. "Do you want to eat first? Or open presents?" he asks.

I rub my hands together and grin. "Presents."

He nods and takes a swig of his soda. "Let's do this."

I place my three presents in front of Dad and then grab the three packages he wrapped for me.

In front of me is one box about the size of a laptop, and two small presents, roughly the size of a cell phone box.

Dad opens his first present revealing a T-shirt with a dad joke on the front. He reads the joke and bursts out laughing. Then he nods to the larger box, wagging his brows. "Open it."

I rip the wrapping paper off, then pull the lid off the box expecting a new laptop. Inside, I find a plane ticket, a warm winter jacket, and a pair of heavy-duty winter boots that look like they could endure Antarctica. I pick up the plane ticket, read the destination, and scrunch my brows together. "Juneau, Alaska?"

Dad nods slowly. "I think you're old enough to go by yourself."

"What's in Juneau?" I ask, eyeing the paper and the jacket.

"Your mother's family. They've been asking about you."

Something inside me snaps and I toss the ticket into the box, then return the top and set it aside. "I hope that's refundable because I'm not going."

Dad's brows shoot upward as if he's alarmed. "Why?"

"Because if they really cared they would've asked about me sixteen years ago."

Dad's lips press into a thin line and he slowly nods. "Maybe we can talk about this later."

"Or maybe we can talk about it never," I mutter, pointing to his gifts. "Open the next one."

He tears open the one that's an envelope and flips through the home-made coupon book I created. "One coupon for taking out the garbage without complaining...one for overseeing a funeral so I can hang out with my friends..." Dad chuckles. "I don't have normal friends. I have you, Irony, Karma, and Kenny—and Mercy if you consider that annoying, bossy woman a friend."

"Maybe you can make a friend. You need a life outside of death. Some-one to keep you grounded in life."

"I have you." Dad's green eyes seem to flash. "You are what keeps me grounded in life. I waited hundreds of years to have you, and you're grow-ing up too fast. I only have a few short years before your childhood is gone, and I refuse to take a single moment for granted."

My cheeks balloon out and I blow out a puff of air. What am I supposed to say to *that*?

Dad flips to the last coupon and bursts out laughing. "One coupon to do all the reaping so I can finally go on a date." Dad chuckles again and wipes his eyes. "Yeah—no. Not gonna happen. I've already got a wife. You met her tonight. Gave her a hug. Remember?"

"In my defense, I hadn't met Mom yet when I made these," I say. She'd been dead sixteen years, ya know? And you hadn't dated a single lady that I can remember. I just wanted you to know you could move on. I want you to have a life after I graduate high school."

Dad pulls the dating coupon from the book, crumples it up, then flicks his wrist. The paper explodes into a ball of fire that consumes the paper into nothingness and then disappears. "Well, now you know."

"Tonight was the first time in sixteen years you've seen her?" I ask.
He nods.

"Isn't that a long time to wait? What if you don't see her for another sixteen years?"

Dad rubs his chin, then leans forward, planting his elbows onto his knees. "I've been alive for hundreds of years. When you get as old as I do, time seems to speed up. You may not understand it now, but the older you get, the more you'll understand that a decade or two is mere minutes—maybe even seconds in the grand scheme of things."

He points to my gifts. "Open another one."

I choose the midnight blue present with foil stars. Inside, it's a keychain with a fob. I'm grinning when I pick it up, then I immediately narrow my eyes at him and scowl. "You're not giving me a hearse are you?"

Dad howls with laughter and shakes his head. "Only because I didn't think of it! Man, that would've been good. No, you're getting a car. You're old enough to drive, and if I can trust you with the secret of being a reaper, I can trust you with your own vehicle. Besides, this might keep you from using your powers to pop to different locations every night."

Dad arches his brow knowingly.

Busted. He must know about my rendezvous with Skye.

He gestures in the direction of the parking lot. "You can check it out after we're done with gifts."

"Cool. Thanks, Dad."

"You've got one more gift," he says, pointing to my last box.

"You have one too." I scowl at him. "Get to work."

He snickers and rips open the final package. It's a photo I took of him and me in the mountains on one of our hikes. The sky is clear and blue, and behind us is a waterfall spraying mist. Our hair is damp and we're grinning from ear to ear. He lifts the picture and stares at it, a tender smile filling his face. "That is a memory worth keeping, isn't it?"

I nod. "I'm lucky you're my dad."

One side of his mouth tips upward. "Thanks, man." Then he gestures to my last box. "The pièce de résistance."

"Better than a car? Nothing's better than a car—as long as it's not a hearse. Then *anything's* better than that."

Inside the box, I find a ring made with a white gold band etched with the same intricate filigree found on my scythe. The top is shaped like a teardrop and looks like it's made of a swirling, sparkling onyx. "So…" I say carefully, trying not to hurt Dad's feelings. "I'm not much of a jewelry guy."

"It's the tears of the devil," Dad says, arching an eyebrow. "I mean. If you don't want it, I'm sure Irony would be more than happy to take it off your hands—"

"No way!" I press the box to my chest, turning partially away from him. "That's so cool, also super creepy, but more cool than creepy."

"And incredibly rare," Dad says. "Only two of these exist. One for each tear the devil has ever shed."

"Seriously?"

"Seriously." Dad nods toward the box. "It was a gift from my father, and now I'm giving it to you."

"How did Grandpa get it?"

"His great-grandfather was the first person appointed to be a reaper when humans came into existence. It's been handed down from father to son ever since."

I stare at the shiny black ring's surface. Though hardly noticeable, a tar-like substance swirls at a snail's pace beneath the surface. I stare at it, mesmerized.

Dad clears his throat. "I wouldn't look at it for too long. Best to keep it in its box and hide it away. The thing still has some pull to it, kind of like that ring from that hobbit show you're obsessed with, though not to that degree."

"Good to know." I close the box holding the ring and blink, shaking my head to clear my thoughts.

"As far as Christmases are concerned, was this a pretty good one?" Dad asks.

"Heck yeah! You're gonna have a hard time topping this next year."

"Or ever," he mutters.

"Or ever."

"Aside from the presents, do you see why Christmas is something to be celebrated?"

"As reapers?" I nod. "I do now. Is it like that every year?"

"Yeah."

"Will I get to see Mom every year at Christmas?"

"I think this was a one-off," Dad says, frowning. "She must've called in a favor to get Eve to let us see her."

My shoulders sag and I nod. "It's still better than nothing."

"Much better than nothing," he agrees. "Merry Christmas, Tim."

"Merry Christmas, Dad."

The End

A Christmas Tale of Gifts, Santa Claus, and Grace

By Kim Roth

It's Christmas Eve again, and the memory comes like a faithful friend. I don't invite it to my thoughts, but I don't need to. It comes softly like snowflakes–beautiful and magical. I look up and watch it descend on me. The memory, with its little-girl wonder and deepening understanding, lands on my conscience like a gift. I was ten years old, and Santa had been coming to my house on Christmas Eve for as long as I could remember.

Santa's Christmas Eve visit to my house was a family tradition, but he didn't come in the usual way. He came early, while my siblings and I were still awake and the house was noisy with the Christmas chaos of happy laughter, bustling people, and a kitchen crowded with extra family and friends. Sometimes he came while we were rushing to wrap a last gift to tuck under the tree before Christmas morning or cleaning the dishes from our Christmas Eve dinner of ham and homemade pies. But Santa always came.

More than once I remember Santa's arrival interrupting us children in our negotiations for who should be Mary or the all-important angel in that year's reenactment of the Nativity story. No one ever wanted to be a bathrobe-wearing shepherd. Being cast as a wise man was definitely a step up, but the angel and Mary were the roles my sister, cousins and I really fought over. Only two female roles for four little girls. It was a recipe for some Christmas drama, for sure. With all the imitation of grown-ups we could muster–as children do who are put in charge of something important–we busily prepared for the Nativity while listening eagerly for Santa's arrival.

"Ho! Ho! Ho!"

I can still feel the thrill of Santa's boisterous call as he flung open the front door and stepped inside, his red velvet bag slung over his shoulder.

"Merry Christmas!" he warmly announced loud enough to greet everyone throughout the house. We children came running from wherever we were.

"Settle down," Dad would remind us with a smirk as we broke all the every-day rules of the house, running past him and through doorways and haphazardly skirting furniture. This was the most thrilling moment of all of Christmas.

"Santa's here! Santa's here!' we yelled as we ran. There would be no "settling down"-- that is until we came face to face with Santa, himself. At the moment of seeing the real Santa—not just one of his helpers—right there in the living room, our exuberance came crashing to a halt as we literally stumbled over each other to claim a seat on the couch. We wanted to sit close enough to see and hear everything but not so close as to have to squirm under Santa's gaze, although we certainly did that when he caught us with his grin. We weren't scared of Santa, but we were awed by him.

He would lumber into the living room and drop his bag full of gifts as if it weighed too much to carry. His red bag was mysteriously misshapen with bulges and corners of unseen packages and surprises. Santa always gave the best gifts on Christmas Eve. These were the ones he brought from the North Pole, not the plastic toys or dolls I had seen in stores the weeks leading up to Christmas day. He brought us girls clothespin dolls with hand-painted faces and miniature dresses or fancy candy suckers Mrs. Claus made especially for us, each with our own name scrolled across in fancy lettering. We savored and licked those suckers for weeks, until my dentist-dad persuaded us to bite into them and be done with it.

I was fascinated by Santa's fluffy white beard and velvety red suit. I giggled to see his belly jiggle when he laughed. And I felt a shy delight by the sparkle in his eyes when he knew I was watching him. Santa was magical to me.

I knew he was the real Santa because he talked to Mom and Dad like old friends and chided my brother, Ryan, about getting into trouble at school again. "You must be relieved to see Santa has a gift for you and not a lump of coal like you probably deserve!" Santa teased with a wink.

But I never understood how he had time to stop by for a visit on a night when he should have been too busy. Occasionally other friends would come by on Christmas Eve to bring our family a special treat or sing a Christmas carol on the doorstep, but this happened only once in a while on Christmas Eve. Santa came every year. I asked friends at school and was surprised that he didn't visit them in the same way.

"I see him at the mall," Tommy explained as he told me why Santa didn't need to stop in to make a personal visit.

"It's probably just one of his helpers anyway," Sarah said. She always seemed a little miffed when I asked her about it, so I eventually stopped.

"How does Santa have time to come to our house and still get all his deliveries made all over the whole world!?" I asked Mom one day in December after surveying my friends at school. I was worried about what she might say but still wanted to know.

"He's pretty great," she said. "And he knows you are too."

"But *how* does he do it?" I persisted asking the question. I wanted to know, even though I was a little afraid of the answer I might get.

"I don't really know," Mom admitted. "I don't think anyone does."

"Sarah thinks it must be one of his helpers who comes. And Matt says there's no such thing as Santa anyway."

"Oh, Santa Claus is real," Mom replied, unfazed. "And he cares about Sarah and Matt just like he cares about you. In fact, Santa loves all the children in the whole world. I'll bet he wishes he could visit everyone before his work starts on Christmas Eve."

Stumped but satisfied enough, I dropped the subject. I was only nine years old, and I was the baby of the family. I was used to feeling this way about the things adults said.

On Christmas Eve that year, I experienced an important right-of-passage: "How about you set the table?" Mom offered me with a wink. I think she knew setting the table was my favorite chore, but I had never been allowed to do it by myself on Christmas Eve before. On that night, we used the special plates.

"With the Christmas plates?" I asked in surprise.

"Of course! You know how to be careful," she assured me with motherly confidence. I was thrilled but bit down my enthusiasm to prove how grown up I could be. I had been given one of the important jobs. Just as Mom showed my sister when I was still too small to help, I carried the china plates–only one at a time–to the table. I carefully centered each plate in front of its chair, exactly two thumb-lengths away from the edge of the table. The plates were white, with a scalloped edge and green and gold trim. I often ran my fingers along the edge, fascinated by the way the bumps felt. In the center of each plate was painted a beautiful Christmas tree decorated with lights, ornaments, and a bright star on top. Packages with ribbons and bows sat waiting under the boughs.

I studied the details etched into the plates as I carried each to its place on the table. I imagined what could be inside each gift, and I felt a growing excitement for Christmas morning and opening the gifts under our tree. Waking from my daydream, I folded each napkin and placed the silverware as Mom had shown me long ago when I was little. Setting the table for Christmas Eve was a privilege, and I would make sure it was done right.

The table looked almost magical when I finished. The special Christmas plates Mom had finally let herself buy after admiring for years at the Cinnamon Bear beckoned everyone to gather. Christmas was here. Those plates had become a family tradition, and–for what felt like my entire nine-year-old lifetime–my little girl heart anticipated eating from those Christmas plates, having cousins over for Christmas Eve, and awaiting Santa's personal visit all in the same breath. That was Christmas.

Forty years later, I still feel heartache as I remember seeing Mom cradle those plates in her arms the day she decided to face the melancholy task of "putting away Christmas" that year. Mom didn't know I was on the stairs that day, watching her. And I didn't see how it happened. I just heard the sobbing and came. Mom was on her knees in front of the china hutch, her arms still wrapped around the festive dishes just washed and dried to put away. Rocking back and forth, pieces of the broken plates began falling from her arms. Her eyes were open, but she looked at nothing and cried without trying to console herself. She scared me. But I couldn't turn away. The plates were still stacked in her arms, but chards of china had fallen to the ground around her and large cracks in the plates made the stack disheveled in her grasp. I stared at the scene, trying to make sense of any of it. Had she carried more than one at a time?

I saw all of this from my hiding place behind the banister. I understood immediately that Christmas would be a little different next year without our Christmas plates. That thought felt sad, but it didn't explain the sensation I felt growing deep inside. I had never heard Mom–or any adult–cry like that before. She must have thought she was alone, and I felt too much to tell her I was there. I stood frozen on the stairs. Watching her, I sensed a sorrow inside I did not understand–a pain I had not felt before. She knelt on the ground holding her broken plates, rocking back and forth as if the steady movement might take her back to a time before.

Even as a nine-year-old girl, I sensed something more important than plates shattered that day. But it was years before I experienced enough life to understand Mom's anguish. Time has taught me that grief and sorrow are occasional companions of love. They bring a burden to love that tries and refines it from anything selfish. Crying over broken plates hurts less than crying about important things. But I didn't know that then.

In the days and months following Christmas that year, there were many hushed conversations in the house. After dinner, Mom and Dad sometimes excused us early from the clean-up work so they could talk alone. Waiting until we had left the kitchen, they lowered their voices so we kids couldn't hear. I tried listening to their quiet, serious-sounding conversations from the living room but had little success.

There were late-night phone calls I strained to hear from my bed. And I frequently heard murmurings through the shared wall between my bedroom and Mom and Dad's room. I rarely understood the words but knew they meant something was wrong. Children always know. Mom was worried and sad. Maybe she was even scared. Dad was disappointed or mad. It was hard to tell the difference.

"Why can't he just get a hold of himself?" I heard Dad ask rhetorically and too loudly one dark winter evening. "He's ruining his life and he's probably going to kill your mother one day!" His words spilled out hot and hung in the air like something ugly no one wanted to look at. "And the girls," gentler now, "I just don't know what's going to come of them." I wasn't sure if Mom was quiet because Dad dared to say something she feared or because she knew I had heard.

Mom was busier than usual that winter, too. She drove us to music lessons, kept order in a full house of seven, served as the Parent-Teacher-Association President at school, and helped Dad at the office. She also spent a lot of time at the hospital.

"Grandma's had a stroke," Mom explained one day.

"What does that mean?" I asked, bracing myself with all the maturity of a just-turned-ten-year-old.

"It means she's very sick and part of her body doesn't work right now. She needs to stay in the hospital for a while, so I'm going to spend as much time there with her as I can."

"Can I come too?"

Mom didn't respond right away. "I'm afraid not, sweetie. Grandma's pretty sick, and the best help she can get is from the doctors and nurses. She'll want to see you as soon as possible, though. She'll want to play Old Maid with you!" Mom tried to reassure both of us.

"Grandma always likes playing cards with me."

I felt something heavy inside as I said the words and looked up to search Mom's face.

"Yes, she does."

Mom smiled but her eyes didn't. "For now, can you be a big girl so I can be with Grandma until she gets better?" Gauging me, Mom paused before she added gently, "Can you help your sister with dinner and go to bed when she says?" I saw the pleading in her eyes. She needed this from me, but I hated when older siblings were put in charge of me.

"Okay," I sighed.

Mom kissed me on the head. "Thanks," she added with another heavy smile. "I'll be back as soon as I can."

❄❄❄

When the warmth of summer finally came, I felt relief. I spent my days playing outside in the yard or riding my bike around the neighborhood and checking in with Mom when I needed a snack. Mom seemed happy and didn't have hushed, serious talks with Dad any more. The light summer air felt fresh and bright. All the dark worries I felt but didn't understand had drifted away with the last of the winter snow. In their place, hope grew up red and yellow like the tulips lining the driveway.

My cousins came to play a lot that summer. Aunt Lola always dropped them off from the driveway. I was delighted to have them to play with, even when they got dropped off without us knowing they were coming. We made the most of every day they came. We played feverishly–often picking up our imaginary games of pretend from wherever we left off the time before–until Aunt Lola suddenly reappeared to take them home. Sometimes she came to the door and talked quietly with Mom for a few minutes before she took the girls home. Other times, she sat in her car in the driveway, and Mom called to us from the back porch to tell us it was time for the girls to go home.

Grandma came to stay with us after she left the hospital that summer.

"Things are going to be harder for Grandma since her stroke," Mom explained, knowing I would need to be patient, "but she'll figure it out. She's too feisty not to."

Mom was right. Grandma was older and slower when she came home, but I loved having her live with us–even though it meant my sister and I had to share a room. Instead of moving Grandma into the spare room in the basement, Mom had Grandma sleep in my bed right next to her room. She stayed close to Grandma during the day, too. Unlike before, though, they didn't spend their time talking and laughing while they worked. Now,

Mom would style Grandma's hair or help her in the bath. Sometimes they just sat together in the new quiet. At dinner time, Mom asked me to help Grandma into the kitchen and all the way to her chair at the table. She rarely helped make dinner now and, when she did, Mom had to watch over her a lot. Grandma didn't knit anymore, either. She couldn't see the ends of the needles well enough. Sometimes I would watch Grandma sitting by herself, staring across the room. Her eyes seemed vacant, and I knew she missed doing the things she used to do.

I played Old Maid with Grandma most days, but it took a lot longer now that she couldn't see very well. She held her cards close to her eyes, but it took some time to find them. Moving her head from side to side, she scanned the space in front of her intently until she could make out each card in her hand. I watched curiously. Teased–and misled–by her persuasive facial expressions as each card came into her view, I confidently drew my next card from her hand.

"It's the Old Maid!" she cackled. "You took the one I hoped you would!"

Grandma loved to win. That hadn't changed since she came home from the hospital. And she never played easy on me–even though I was the baby. I loved her for that. She bellowed her sharp, loud laugh every time I drew the Old Maid from her hand. And, even though I tried the same persuasive tricks on her, she didn't fall prey very often. We rarely finished a game with the Old Maid in her hand.

Grandma had always been a great storyteller, and I think she was even better after her stroke made her eyes bad. I would cozy up next to her on the couch and ask her to tell me the story of "The Three Billy Goats Gruff."

"Again!?" She pretended to be tired from the frequent request.

I never felt too grown up to hear her stories. I giggled as she made a different voice for each goat and walked her fingers across my knee to show

how the goats went "trip, trap" across the imaginary bridge. She never left out an animated detail—no matter how many times she repeated the story.

I was fascinated by Grandma's stories, especially the ones she had lived. And did she ever have stories to tell! None of my friends' Grandmas rode motorcycles or had ever gone hang-gliding! Grandma talked about her grand adventures as much as anyone would listen. Truthfully, she loved to brag. She bragged about the things she had done and the quick-witted things she had said. If she ever told off someone she was unhappy with, we were all sure to hear about it. And she always gave her cackle-laugh as she finished the story. She had a tongue like a whip and was proud of it! Sometimes this embarrassed my mom.

"Mother," Mom would scold. But Grandma thought it was fun.

"It's the Laramie in me," she excused herself. Mom would smile but shake her head when Grandma took to feeling sassy like this.

Grandma bragged about lots of things. She bragged about still having all of her own teeth at her age. "Thanks to your dad being such a good dentist," she was quick to add. She bragged to her friends about us grand-kids. She bragged about being the only lady at the senior center all the men wanted to dance with. And she bragged about being able to snap her gum.

"I really made those nurses crazy with my gum-snapping," she boasted. "Said they'd never known anyone who could snap it so loud. And so many times!"

Near the middle of summer, my cousins came for a sleepover and didn't leave for weeks. These were blissful days. We shared the same Grandma, so there were more of us to play Old Maid and listen to stories. I moved out of the room I had had to share with my too-grown-up-to-play-pretend sister to the downstairs family room where my cousins and I built forts and slept in sleeping bags on the floor. Sometimes we took our sleeping bags outside to sleep in the backyard. During the day, my cousins and I spent hours playing in the backyard. We acted out all kinds of elaborate pretend stories we imagined, using the apple tree, swing set, and vegetable garden as our backdrop.

Mom was busy with phone calls and sitting with Grandma that summer, so I relished in her slight distraction which freed me from practicing the violin and doing my chores around the house. Instead, my cousins and I sprinted bare-foot through sprinklers set in the soft grass, shrieked as we ran from the innocent daddy-long-leg spiders we found in the cool shade, and listened for the thrilling song of the ice cream truck as it drove slowly down the street.

Winston, our old blue-eyed Alaskan Malamute, would occasionally lift his head to watch us from his usual place under the apple tree. During the school year, his vigil included lumbering to the edge of the driveway to greet me as I walked home from school. On warm summer afternoons such as these, however, a brief ears-at-attention scan across the yard from his spot of shade easily confirmed that everything was in order. Winston would then roll contentedly back onto his side to sleep in the long grass under the apple tree.

The cousins stayed for so long I began to wonder why, but I hesitated to ask for fear it would somehow end my carefree summer. When I finally noticed that Mom was regularly washing their clothes with mine, and about the time we girls had our first argument, I felt brave enough to ask.

"Uncle Scotty had to go away for a while," Mom explained, "so Aunt Lola has a lot of extra things to do."

"Like what?" I stood next to Mom as she cut cheese for sandwiches on the wooden pull-out cutting board. She cut a few more slices. "Well, she has two jobs now so can't be home very much. I don't think the girls would have a very happy summer being alone every day. And sometimes, Aunt Lola works at night, too."

"Oh." I watched Mom turn to open the cupboard, looking for bread. "Why does Aunt Lola have to work so much?" This all seemed very strange to me. In Mom's silence I continued, "Why did Uncle Scotty have to go away?"

This must have been a hard question because Mom didn't say anything for a long time. She stopped searching in the cupboard and turned to me. Slowly, she lowered to a crouch to look eye-level at me. This was serious. She reached for my hand.

"Uncle Scotty did a very bad thing. He's been doing it for a while, I guess," Mom answered carefully. "So he's had to be away from his family for a long time."

"Oh." Wishing I hadn't asked but still not understanding, I pressed on. "Where did he go?"

There was another long pause. Mom sighed and dropped her eyes from mine. She pressed her lips sideways in that way she always did when she was thinking. Lifting her eyes again, she carefully tucked my long hair behind my shoulder. "He's in prison."

"Prison?" I barely whispered. "I thought only really bad people went there."

"Uncle Scotty's not a bad person. We love Uncle Scotty. But he has done some bad things and needs help."

"And the people in prison will help him?"

"Well, it's a place to start." Mom looked at me intently. She was holding both of my hands now. "We can help by letting the girls play at our house for as long as Aunt Lola needs. I'm sure they miss their dad a lot."

"Ok." I looked down. "But sometimes I miss the way things used to be."

Mom shifted to her knees to hold me close. "Me, too."

❋❋❋

Just before school started again, Aunt Lola arrived to take the girls home. She parked the car in the driveway and came inside for a bit to help them pack their things. We took down our sleeping fort, and they said goodbye to Grandma.

Almost immediately after my cousins left, the chore chart was again placed prominently in the kitchen, and I resumed practicing the violin every day Mom remembered to tell me. Eventually, even Grandma went back home to "see if she'd be okay on her own." Mom and Dad talked a lot about Uncle Scotty and the girls now, and they didn't change the subject when I came into the room. Uncle Scotty would be getting out of prison soon.

"I hope he can get some work lined up," Dad worried out loud after dinner one evening. He was adding logs to the wood-burning stove behind his usual seat at the kitchen table. We had a furnace, but Dad loved the warmth of a fire in the cool fall evenings.

Finished stoking the fire, Dad closed the glass door and moved into the living room where he could watch the burning logs through the two-sided fireplace. He settled onto the couch near where I was busy with coloring pages and my older sister worked on math homework. Mom pulled a chair close to the fire where she could admire the flames through the glass. She hefted the afghan she was perpetually knitting onto her lap.

"I don't know what he's going to do," Mom finally replied to Dad's comment still hanging in the air. Dad picked up the newspaper waiting on the lamp table next to him. Mom looked across the room at Dad. "Lola's pretty worried about Christmas, too."

"Christmas? They need to worry about putting bread on the table, not Christmas." Dad spoke but didn't put down the newspaper.

"You're right, but it's hard not being able to do something for your own children." Mom's knitting needles clicked quietly in the space between them. "I know that's how I would feel."

"I know you would. But Scott hasn't exactly put their family in normal circumstances." Dad looked over the top of his glasses and the newspaper to catch Mom's eyes. She didn't seem to notice and kept knitting. "What are you conjuring up?" he asked like a warning. "I'm concerned about giving them more money than we already have. I mean, at what point are we just enabling him?" Mom kept knitting. "And I don't think we should underestimate the expenses we have ahead with James and Ryan going to college soon."

"I agree. But maybe there's something we can do–just for the girls." Mom didn't look up from her knitting, but hastily added, "Not anything expensive."

Nothing more was said of it. The room was quiet for a time. Dad's newspaper rustled as he turned the large pages over his lap. Mom's needles clicked along as she occasionally said a number aloud, counting stitches. Dad commented to Mom about a few wedding announcements he saw in the paper. Mom seemed pleased to hear about the new couples and cheered when she finished another row of the growing blanket. A ball of yarn sat next to Mom, feeding her needles, and the ever-growing afghan lay strewn across her lap, reaching for the floor.

"It's probably about bedtime for you two girls, isn't it?" Dad asked as he folded the paper and set it on the coffee table in front of him. It wasn't really a question.

"I guess," I responded slowly for both of us. I didn't like having to go to bed earlier than my teenage brothers who were probably downstairs watching TV.

"I'll be there to tuck you in after you brush your teeth," Mom assured us.

I had a hard time falling asleep that night. I lay awake in the quiet darkness, thinking about Christmas. I tried imagining what I would put on my wishlist or which of my sibling's names I might draw to buy a gift for. I forced myself to picture Christmas morning—sitting around the Christmas tree, opening presents with my family. But the heaviness of Mom and Dad's disagreement sat on my mind, and when I thought of Uncle Scotty, everything was gray.

Over the next few days, my thoughts wandered back to everyday things until I noticed Mom was still thinking about Christmas. She taped a homemade skull and crossbones sign to her bedroom door, which meant all of us kids were supposed to stay out so we didn't spoil a Christmas surprise. And I heard her occasionally working her sewing machine after my bedtime. I laid in bed listening to the motor start and stop, start and stop. She was probably making new matching nightgowns for my sister and me. But I hoped it was a new dress for my dolls. Christmas-time kept Mom busy with magical secrets, and this year looked to be no different.

I stayed busy that Christmas season, too. I memorized all my lines for the school Christmas play, practiced carols on the violin, and wondered what I could give my big brothers if I drew one of their names for our sibling gift-exchange. I never knew what to give a big brother who was so old and seemed like another dad to me–telling me what to do and pointing out that my sister and I never helped weed the garden.

"The girls," my brothers would complain to Dad, "never work in the yard!" It bugged me the way they referred to my sister and me as "the girls."

I knew enough to know they didn't use it as a term of endearment. My big brothers seemed bossy to me, but I admit I knew they loved me. That was the year Ryan surprised me with a wooden tic-tac-toe game he spent two months carving in his shop class. I wished I had given him such a gift.

In fact, that was the year we all gave homemade gifts for Christmas.

"What do you mean you and Dad aren't spending money on presents this year?" James sounded upset. I sat on the bench in front of the big kitchen window, watching the snow blow across the driveway.

"Dad and I have decided we want to do things differently this year. Of course, you can do what you'd like with your own money, but Dad and I won't be spending our money to give gifts this Christmas." James didn't say anything but kept loading the dishwasher. "It might be good for all of us to put more thought than money into our gifts, anyway."

James didn't seem so sure. All of us kids had already been creating our wish lists—my sister and I from the things we'd seen advertised in the commercials during Saturday morning cartoons, and my brothers from the things their friends had or talked about wanting.

But Mom was undaunted by James' obvious irritation. As Christmas drew closer, she was busier and looked happier than ever. She definitely had a secret. I heard her sewing machine working every night after she tucked me into bed, and she was doing a lot of Christmas shopping for someone who said we weren't spending money on gifts this year. Once, she brought me into her bedroom and asked me to keep my eyes closed while she had me try on something she was making. She needed to see how the sizing was coming along. I felt the fabric go over my head. It didn't feel like it would be a nightgown. The excitement was almost too much, but I managed to keep my eyes closed until she turned me around and walked me out of the room.

❄❄❄

Two weeks before Christmas, Mom told me we would have a busy afternoon when I got home from school that day. It sounded more ominous than exciting–I assumed she meant we would need to spend a lot of time practicing to catch up before violin lessons that week. I hadn't spent much time playing the violin since we had been so busy making gifts and preparing for Christmas. It turned out that making gifts was more fun to me than going shopping for them, and I was always eager for the times when Mom was too busy to think to remind me to practice the violin. Looking back now, I wish I hadn't made this so hard on her.

"What do we need to do today?" I asked as I pulled on my boots to walk to school.

"Well, Uncle Scotty came home a few days ago. So I'd like to go see him. Your sister is babysitting for the Olsens after school. I thought maybe you could come with me and play with your cousins while I talk with Uncle Scotty and Aunt Lola. I know you haven't played with the girls for a long time." This was definitely better than the busy plan I had feared.

"Uncle Scotty gets to come home for Christmas? That's great! Holly and Jill will be so excited!"

"Yes, we're all really glad about that. I'll bet the girls and Aunt Lola are especially happy. After we visit with them, I'd like to go shopping for a few minutes." Mom noticed my suspicious look. "Not long," she added. Mom often added errands to our list of things to do when we were already out of the house. "I just want to pick up a few gifts for your cousins. I thought it would be fun to get them some things for Christmas. Maybe you can help me pick out something special?" This sounded like a lot more fun than some of Mom's "quick stops" to the bank or grocery store. I didn't mind shopping if it meant looking at dolls.

"Ok!" I agreed, happy that it sounded like another afternoon with no time to practice the violin.

"Great. I'll pick you up after school, then."

I was so excited to play with Holly and her little sister, Jill, when we got to their house later that day, I didn't even notice Uncle Scotty standing near the front door.

"Well, hello, Kimberli." He spoke quietly, but his silky voice startled me. He looked down at me, his eyes opened expectantly and too wide.

"Oh hi, Uncle Scotty." I reached up to give him a hug. He was tall and felt thinner than when I hugged my dad, or even my brothers. Longing to join the pretend I knew was waiting for me with my cousins, I forced myself into learned politeness and stayed in the awkward adult world until dismissed. I looked around in the thick silence, hoping for an escape. The front room was messy. The floor was littered with boxes—some closed, some open with contents spilling out. The room was empty of furniture, except for one brown couch. It was the one I had seen in all the houses they moved to. They never stayed very long. I always thought moving seemed exciting since I had lived in the same house my entire life. Holly said she was tired of always going to new schools, though.

Finally, Mom took a few steps toward the couch and slid a pile of clothes to the side so she could sit next to the heap of socks and shirts.

"I'm glad to see you, too." Scotty compensated for my bashfulness. He moved a box to sit with Mom, and Aunt Lola came in from the kitchen.

"Hi, Kimi!" Aunt Lola looked tired but always wore a smile for me. "You look like you've grown taller since the summer!" She looked me over for confirmation and grinned. "The girls are down the hall," she added. And there was my out.

Later that afternoon, there were lots of hugs at the door as we left. Uncle Scotty kept reassuring Mom. "We're fine," he said. "I'll find work, and things are going to be better." Mom searched his face. Uncle Scotty laughed at Mom like she was taking this all too seriously. "Really. I'm not going to need that stuff anymore." Then, in a final attempt to persuade her, he straightened his shoulders and stood a little taller. "I'm a changed man." Sarcasm dripped off the words.

Mom studied Uncle Scotty. Her smile came, slow and deliberate. "I'll bring some dinner by tomorrow," she said, turning to Aunt Lola.

With resolute reassurance in her voice, Lola nodded. "Thank you."

Mom stayed quiet as we drove away. I sat thinking about the fort we built in the room Holly and Jill shared. We had found plenty of boxes to use. They were scattered, half-unpacked, throughout the house. I thought I would feel happy to play with my cousins again but couldn't help feeling the heaviness of a worry I didn't understand.

At the store, Mom had me try on a few things so she could see how they would fit Holly and Jill.

"Oh! Look!" I exclaimed when we made our way to the toy department. "It's the new Cabbage Patch Dolls! They're so cute! Sarah's asking for one for Christmas. She wants a boy with a pacifier. She already has two girls. I think they're twins."

"Wow." Mom studied the dolls. She picked one box at a time off the shelf and peered through its plastic covering to see the details of each doll. "That's a lot of dolls for one little girl."

"Well, it would make playing house more fun. And you could get lots of cute outfits for them to share! I hope *I* get a new Cabbage Patch Doll for Christmas." I said the last part a little timidly–not sure how much parents compared wishlist notes with Santa.

Mom didn't say anything for several minutes while she looked at a few more dolls. Then, as if speaking out loud mid-thought, she said, "We're not buying gifts for Christmas this year, though. All our gifts will be homemade."

"We're not buying gifts?" I repeated her exact words as if they were a question, not entirely sure what they meant.

"Uh-huh." Mom didn't take her eyes off the doll in her hand.

"But why?" When Mom didn't answer, I persisted. "Does that mean we won't get presents from Santa?"

After another pause, Mom put the boxed doll she'd been studying back on the shelf. "Well, Daddy and I want to do something to help Uncle Scotty's family have a nice Christmas. We decided to save the money we would have spent on our family and use it to buy gifts for Holly, Jill, and even Uncle Scotty and Aunt Lola."

"But then how will *we* have a nice Christmas?" I was embarrassed by the quick surge of anger I felt but didn't have time to stop the words from tumbling out. I was dangerously close to tears, and I think Mom knew it. A hug would have been too much so Mom quietly reassured me from where she stood.

"We'll have a lovely Christmas." Her voice was gentle but sure. "We're going to make special gifts for each other and eat special foods. And we'll all be together! This will be a very happy Christmas. I promise."

Not wanting to risk crying in public, I was relieved when Mom said we would finish our shopping another day, and we drove home.

The rest of the days leading up to Christmas were a busy blur. I accepted Mom's offer to help me think of gift ideas I could make for my siblings. I finally decided to make a coupon booklet of things I could do to help my big brother, James, with his chores, but I admit to hoping he never actually took me up on it. I didn't really want to make his bed for him or take his turn doing the dishes. I did not make a coupon to weed his rows in the garden that summer—just in case. Luckily, my 4th grade teacher, Mrs. Caldwell, planned an art activity of making a pottery sun-catcher. I was quite proud of mine and decided to give it to Mom and Dad as their Christmas gift. They both seemed pleased and Dad hung it prominently in front of the window over the kitchen sink. I made a hair bow for my sister at a church children's activity. I chose a yellow ribbon since that was her favorite color.

After school one day, Mom said, "I need a little help wrapping presents this afternoon." I loved wrapping presents for Mom. She always fussed over each one I wrapped, so I felt like I did a really good job. Mom worked hard for a good surprise and made sure she already had the gifts hidden inside boxes so all I wrapped was a nondescript box. I rarely knew what was inside or who it was for. Often on Christmas morning, I realized I had wrapped my own presents!

"Today we're wrapping presents for Uncle Scotty's family," Mom announced as she led me and my sister into her room. It was exciting to be invited past the threshold of all Christmas secrets. My sister and I wrapped a sweater for Aunt Lola, some new pants for Uncle Scotty, and a pretty pink dress for Jill. Pink was her favorite color, so I knew she would love it. It wasn't until Mom pulled out the new Cabbage Patch Doll for Holly that I began to feel the jealousy rise up hot inside me. Mom watched me carefully. Not daring to say anything, I chose a wrapping paper and reached for the scissors, focusing hard to see through my watery eyes. My sister taped a bow onto the package she was wrapping and only looked up at me when she thought I wouldn't notice.

"How will we deliver the presents so they don't know who they're from?" I asked, wanting to fill the empty space made by our silence. I was annoyed that my mom and sister kept looking at me like I was fragile.

"I think we'll ask Santa to do it. Maybe he can visit them on Christmas Eve?"

I pressed tape onto the green paper I had chosen to wrap Holly's new doll.

"We get to have him come to our house every year," Mom continued. "Maybe the girls would like to have a special visit from Santa at their own house on Christmas Eve?" Spoken gently, the words still hung like shards of something broken, suspended in the air.

Willing my tears to keep from spilling over, I said nothing but pretended to look through the collection of fancy bows we had saved from previous Christmases. Something about the way she said it made me know it meant that Santa would not be coming to our house on Christmas Eve that year. He would take his red velvet bag of magical gifts to Holly and Jill's house. How did Mom have anything to do with where Santa made his Christmas Eve visit, anyway? I bit down on my jaw as I realized the truth I had been dreading. I shook my head against hot tears, knowing I had to accept my new reality about Santa Claus.

❄❄❄

Unsure if I felt more dread or anticipation for it, Christmas Eve finally came. Mom and I met Santa in Uncle Scotty's neighborhood in the early evening. We parked down the street and out of sight from the house as the last of the sun's light stretched across the snowdrifts left behind in the wind-blown yards. House lights were beginning to peek out through drawn curtains and a few Christmas lights decorated the barren trees in front of houses. I opened the car door and climbed out. It was cold and quiet. I stood on the sidewalk, feeling the brisk air and taking in the stillness left after a winter storm leaves its blanket of white. A car drove slowly down the street, occasionally veering right to see house numbers. Finally, it pulled up to the curb and parked behind our car.

Santa saw me watching him and waved at me through the front windshield. He stepped out of the car–already wearing his velvety, red suit. Mom had never explained how this would happen, but I wasn't surprised to see Santa arrive by station wagon. I grinned–cautious, but feeling a budding pride at being part of the grown-up club.

"Merry Christmas, Kimi!" Santa called to me as he stepped out onto the street. Amazed by the familiarity of his dancing eyes and warm voice, I studied his face. "Do you have the gifts you want me to give your cousins?" Relief washed through me. He knew that I knew, and neither of us had to pretend.

"Yes, we do," I responded–proud now and encouraged. "The trunk is full of presents!"

"Ho! Ho! Well, it looks like you've been a very busy girl this Christmas!" I blushed at his praise. "Thanks for letting me deliver your gifts, Kimi. This will be a special Christmas for your cousins."

I helped Santa fill his bag with our gifts for Uncle Scotty's family, and Mom stacked the food and Christmas treats into a box. The trunk now empty and Santa's arms full, we watched him walk down the street to their house. Mom put her arm around me. We stood silently out of sight on the sidewalk until we heard what we were listening for.

"Ho! Ho! Ho!" Santa exclaimed when the door opened. Little girl squeals and giggles rang through the night air like jingle bells, the joyful chorus singing across the silence of the snow. I stayed quiet, aware of a Christmas magic I hadn't known before.

"Mom!" Holly called out, "Santa's here. He actually came!"

Christmas morning came with a fresh dusting of soft, white snow. Although Christmas Eve had been a change from tradition without Santa's visit or Christmas plates to make our dinner special, I felt a lingering warmth inside from sharing Santa with my cousins. It was an unexpected, new kind of Christmas delight.

Wearing the homemade nightgowns Mom gave us after Christmas Eve dinner, my sister and I woke early and rushed downstairs to coax our brothers out of bed. With sleepy eyes and pretended disinterest, they finally meandered into the family room about the time Mom and Dad came down to join us. James and Ryan were both wearing the new pajamas Mom had made for them.

We took our time opening gifts that morning. Unlike Christmases of the past, we were more excited to see how our gifts to each other were received than to open gifts ourselves. I could hardly stand the anticipation I felt watching my brothers and sister slowly open, with exaggerated care, a gift I had made and wrapped for them. As soon as the moment of reveal came, I launched into an excited, lengthy explanation of how I made the gift and why I thought the color or design was just right for the person. We all felt this enthusiasm for giving our homemade gifts.

Mom surprised me with a new doll. Instead of buying the store-bought Cabbage Patch Doll I had hoped for all those weeks ago, Mom made this doll herself—modeling it after the one I had admired in the store. Every detail was stitched into the doll. She had long hair made of yellow yarn, which was swooped into two ponytails high on her head. Embroidery floss filled in her blue eyes. Thread gathered the fabric of her hands and feet to form little fingers and toes. And Mom even remembered to stitch a dimple into her cheek. I turned her around and around, inspecting all of her details. She was a little lumpy in places and one arm was slightly longer than the other.

Mom giggled nervously as she watched me. I giggled, too. The doll was imperfect and misshapen. She looked a little silly. But even my little-girl-self knew that this doll meant more than the perfect ones at the store. I hugged my new doll and handed her to my sister who wanted a turn to admire her. Mom winked at me as a flash of relief crossed her face.

Grandma had come to be with us for Christmas that year. She usually did, but that year I felt especially grateful. Losing her eyesight had been hard on Grandma physically and emotionally. I knew my mom worried about her, and so I worried, too. I was happy, even relieved, she felt up to coming for a visit. I didn't mind giving up my bedroom again because Christmas wouldn't have felt the same without her with us. Already, the holiday had been a little different since Uncle Scotty and Aunt Lola didn't bring the girls over like they usually did on Christmas Eve. So Grandma being there brought some normalcy to Christmas.

Once gifts were opened and we finished breakfast, I asked Mom if we could please go to Holly and Jill's house. I wanted to hear about their visit from Santa and what they thought of their gifts. Mom said she would love to visit with Scotty and Lola, so we decided to go and wish them a "Merry Christmas." Grandma wanted to see Scotty and Lola and the girls before Mom drove her back home, too. We hadn't heard from the family for a few days, but Mom reassured me that they were probably so happy to have their dad home and to be together as a family again, that they hadn't thought to accept our annual invite to come for Christmas Eve dinner.

After the short drive across town, Mom, Grandma and I stood on the front step at Uncle Scotty's house. I grinned as I imagined Santa's surprise visit on this very step just the day before. We waited for several minutes after ringing the bell. Finally, Aunt Lola came to the door. Her eyes seemed dull.

"Oh, hi." Her voice was flat. "I didn't know you were coming."

"We just thought we'd stop by for a minute to say 'Merry Christmas.' We missed you at Christmas Eve dinner. And Grandma wanted to come see the girls before I take her back home tomorrow." We stood awkwardly on the doorstep while Mom fumbled through an explanation of why we had come.

"It's not really a good time." She stood in the doorway, with the door pulled mostly closed, resting on her back. "Scott's not feeling well."

Just then Uncle Scotty came from behind Aunt Lola and pulled the door open wide. Talking a bit too enthusiastically and a lot too loudly, he said, "Well, hello, Sis! Come on in!"

Lola's eyes gave away her surrender, and she moved aside so we could step into the living room. It was unchanged from the mess of moving in. Only a bit of scattered wrapping paper was new. "Still trying to get unpacked," Lola explained uneasily.

"Oh, this!? No problem!" shouted Uncle Scotty. "I can have these boxes unpacked in no time." He opened a box to reveal books inside. Grabbing one side of the now opened lid, he jerked the box close to the wall, sliding it across the floor and crashing it into several boxes on its way. He looked around frantically. "What? No bookshelf?" He announced sarcastically. "No problem. We're unpacking, so that's what I'll do." He reached into the box and pulled out a stack of books. He piled them haphazardly onto the floor. "Is this better for everyone? I just want to make everyone happy."

"What's Daddy doing?" Holly had come down the hall. She stood at the edge of the living room, looking at Uncle Scotty

"Oh he's just excited." Aunt Lola's voice sounded feeble. "Don't worry, sweetie. He'll quiet down soon enough."

"I don't like it when Daddy's like this." Jill had come down the hall and was hiding behind Holly, wearing the nightgown Mom had made her for Christmas.

I stared at Uncle Scotty, forgetting to be polite. Unsure of why Uncle Scotty was acting so strange, and a little scared by the way he aggressively unpacked books onto a bookshelf that wasn't there, I stood frozen, watching.

"Lola, can I help you unpack a few boxes in the kitchen while Grandma watches the girls play in the bedroom?"

"Yes, please." Lola whispered her response and moved without looking into the kitchen. Grandma took my arm, and we followed Holly back into her bedroom. After carefully closing the door behind us, Holly picked up her new Cabbage Patch Doll and sat next to Jill on the bed. Both girls looked up at us with wide eyes.

"Daddy took some pills to help him work better again, didn't he? I hate it when he does that." Holly wrapped one arm around Jill, hugging her Cabbage Patch Doll on her lap with the other. Grandma moved uneasily to take a seat on the edge of the bed but gave no response. I studied Grandma's sad eyes. They seemed vacant. Not knowing what else to do, I sat down on the floor. We could still hear Uncle Scotty. I couldn't make out all of his words, but he was yelling, and there were random loud crashing sounds. On the floor next to me I noticed a few clothes for Holly's new doll and suggested we dress her up. Holly didn't say anything but nodded and handed the doll to me.

Suddenly the door opened and Mom appeared in the bedroom doorway. Her mouth was tight and her eyes wide. She scanned the room until she saw my cousins sitting rigidly on their bed beside Grandma. Quickly, she moved across the room and knelt next to Holly. All her determination melted as she paused, then began to speak gently. "Sweetie, stay in here to play with Jill for a while, will you? Your Dad's going to tire out soon. You're safe, and your mom is here. Your Dad just needs a little time. He's going to get better, though." Holly held Mom's eyes with her own and nodded once. "Your Dad and Mom both love you. I love you, too."

Mom stood then.

"Mother, it's time to go." And turning to me, she added, "I'm sorry, Kimi." But her shaky voice failed to reassure me the way her words were meant to. "I think it would be better to come by another day." I saw the panic nearly spilling over her eyes and got up from my spot on the floor.

"Oh, you won't need to come by another day." Uncle Scotty was yelling again from the living room. "We won't need any help from you. We've never needed any help from you! I'll have this whole mess unpacked in no time." Mom led Grandma and me urgently toward his rampage and to the front door to leave. He looked up at us with both fury and pleading in his eyes as we hurried toward our escape. Aunt Lola did not come out of the kitchen. Uncle Scotty stared at us with wide, threatening eyes. "I'll never need any help from you. Just get out!" he screamed. "And don't come back. Ever!"

I didn't dare to look at Uncle Scotty as he threw his furious words at us. We stepped outside into the cold. Without a word back at Uncle Scotty, Mom closed the door behind us. For a brief moment, we stood on the front step. Mom's hand shook a little on my back. I heard her exhale. Still huddled close, the three of us began moving toward the car. Grandma held my arm as she carefully navigated the steps in her newly darkened world. I held on to her tight, worried she would fall. We were almost to the car.

Abruptly, the door was ripped open and more furious shouting flew out.

"What have you ever done for us, anyway!?" Uncle Scotty stood in the shadow of the front door he had flung open to deliver this last barrage of rage. I looked back. He was just a silhouette now. His arms hung at his side. His hands were shaking and his chest heaved.

Mom didn't look back. Her now steady hand was on my back, urging me forward. Keeping Grandma between us, she led us the last few steps to the car.

"Are we ever going to tell them the gifts were from us?" I asked in the silence as Mom drove down the dark street.

"Would you like to?"

Feeling more grown up from her question, I sat a little straighter as I looked out the window. "No. It seems better this way," I decided aloud.

A few quiet minutes later, we pulled into the driveway of our home. Dad had already turned on the Christmas lights in the front yard. They were beautiful. Shining through what otherwise felt like a dark, cold night, they seemed unusually bright–glistening across the light dusting of new snow. The lights decorated our house in a soft glow and stood against the dark night, like the hope of Christmas day itself.

The car came to a stop. I imagined the rest of our family waiting for us inside. My sister was probably drawing. James and Ryan were likely doing something to purposely annoy her. And Dad would be stoking the fire. I held onto Grandma to keep her safe as we walked from the car, then I opened the front door while Mom helped her inside. Happy sounds came pouring out of the house.

"Mom! When's dinner?" yelled James from downstairs. Dad was in the kitchen by the fireplace. He quickly skimmed a page of the newspaper before he crumpled it to toss into the fire.

"How's Uncle Scotty and the family?" Dad asked as the three of us walked past to the living room.

With a grace I still aspire to, Mom's assuring answer was simple: "The girls loved their gifts from Santa and are doing fine. Lola is a little worn down and grateful for any help." Mom settled Grandma onto the couch in the living room. "It hasn't been a good day for Scott, though."

I heard Dad shift in his chair in the kitchen. He crumpled another sheet of newspaper for the fire and sighed audibly. "Oh dear."

Mom asked me to stay with Grandma and called to everyone else to come help make dinner. Grandma laid down and stretched out the length of the couch. She immediately closed her eyes. She did not want to talk or play Old Maid. I looked around the room, not sure how to take care of a Grandma who was resting.

Images of the day began to come to my mind. I thought of opening homemade gifts with my family; I thought of the ham Mom had in the crockpot for our Christmas dinner. I saw Holly holding the Cabbage Patch Doll I had once envied as she sat with her arm around her little sister on their shared bed. I saw Uncle Scotty with his wild eyes. I felt Mom's strength as she placed her arm on my back to guide me forward down the steps of Uncle Scotty's house. And I heard Grandma's tired, sad voice asking to go home.

Grandma looked peaceful now, resting on the couch. I crept toward her, watching for any movement. She lay perfectly still. An impish idea crossed my mind and, without another thought, I reached out and waved my hand feverishly in front of her face. Nothing. She didn't move. Curious what might happen, I then waved both hands—as fast as I could without bumping her nose—in front of her face. She stayed perfectly still. I studied her, a little worried. But then, I saw it. The left side of her mouth turned up ever so slightly. An almost imperceptible smile flashed across her lips. She knew I was playing with her, taking care of her in my child-like way. And she was playing with me, taking care of me in her grandma-like way. I loved my Grandma.

And then I felt sad because I thought of Uncle Scotty. He had not been a good son to Grandma today. There must have been other days, too. I thought of the hushed conversations I had heard and not heard over the past year. I remembered when Mom told me Uncle Scotty was in prison. Poor Grandma! That must have been a hard day. I remembered the worry I felt when Grandma was in the hospital after her stroke. Did Grandma have a stroke because her son had to go to prison? Grandma would never see well again. Maybe she would never knit again. Probably there would be more hard days ahead.

Things my adults had said came to my mind as I began fidgeting with objects in the room. I twisted the lamp shade and remembered Dad's frustrated outbursts about Uncle Scotty and how the things he did might end up hurting Grandma. I straightened yesterday's newspaper still sitting on the lamp table and heard Mom reminding me that "we love Uncle Scotty." Her eyes were tired when she said the words, but even in the moment I knew she meant them.

I noticed our Nativity set displayed prominently on the table in front of the couch. The figure of the shepherd had been bumped and was angled away from the baby Jesus. All the other figures were turned toward Jesus. I reached for the errant shepherd, intending to turn him back toward the infant Savior but paused. Maybe our little Nativity display was just as it should be. Jesus's arms were still opened for all–no matter which direction each figure faced. Mom had shown me His kind of love that day.

I could hear Mom in the kitchen. All my siblings were gathered around her. She was assigning jobs to make dinner together. I heard the crackle of new logs igniting in flame and looked through the fireplace door to see Dad sitting on the other side. He saw me and waved through the fireplace before closing the glass door. He stood, and I heard him ask if he could peel the potatoes. I felt the warmth of family and Christmas and faith. It had been a different kind of Christmas, but it was just as Mom had promised—a lovely Christmas.

Grandma was resting peacefully. Her steady, slow breathing gave away that she had drifted into sleep. She looked content. I heard Mom laughing at one of James's stories as they worked in the kitchen. She was happy—amazingly, and sincerely happy.

I looked back at the Nativity and the figure of the baby Jesus.

"God is the best Giver, though." I suddenly heard Santa's words in my mind as audibly and fresh as though they were being spoken again that day. He had said those words in my living room the year before, when he came on Christmas Eve. I sat timidly on his lap, and he handed me the most beautiful, handmade apron a little girl could ever hope to have for herself. Santa Claus—I believed then—and my mom—I was now beginning to understand—gave such wonderful gifts.

"You're the best, Santa!" I hugged him unabashedly. He looked at me with Christmas magic in his eyes and smiled warmly, like he meant it. "It's God who gives the greatest gifts." Santa looked at me earnestly and lowered his voice to nearly a whisper. "He gave us His Son."

It had been a year since I heard those words. Yet, like watching a single snowflake fall slowly and silently from the sky, understanding finally landed on my open palm—gently and almost imperceptibly. It was starting to snow outside now—a beautiful kind of Christmas snow. I turned to watch out the window as soft, white flakes began to cascade down through the glow of Christmas lights and street lights in front of the house.

"Kimi?" Mom's soft voice pulled me from my vigil.

"Yes?"

"It looks like you took good care of Grandma. I'm glad she's resting. Are you ready for dinner?"

I nodded.

"Me too." Mom hugged me then. "Merry Christmas, Kimi."

"Yes, it is," I said as I realized it, "a very Merry Christmas."

SEASONS GRIEVING

BY SHANNA L. K. MILLER

Seasons Grieving

The nativity of her life
was a joyous culmination
of love and longing.

Her death, so young,
a candle blown out
much, much too soon.

I wore my grief for her
like a prickly wreath,
heavy around my neck.

I would not allow
any light to pierce
this hollow heart.

My shiny tinsel of hope
lay unhung,
tarnishing in its box.

Bereft; deaf to them,
no bells of joy
rang out for me.

Just numbing
dull pain.
Every. Day.

Finally, tentatively,
I sought relief
outside of myself.

Reaching to, lifting others,
I found and grew
into my own healing.

Though it still pricks me,
I chose to remove and
tuck my wreath of grief away.

I knew its season
may come again;
but not today!

DOORBELL DITCHING WITH OLLY T

BY KATHRYN ROSENBAUM

The Plan

"All right, Olly T. Do you remember the plan?"

Olly's dark eyes squinted as he surveyed the modest home through the car window. The curtains were closed, but a warm orange glow outlined the windows of the front room.

"Is it dark enough? Is she going to see me?"

"You've got this. Just stick to the plan, buddy."

He nodded.

"Do you remember the plan?" Quincy pursed her lips and waited for her young friend to recite it back to her. She didn't want to rush him. After all, this experience was for him, as much as Grandma Berty. But it was important to get it right.

After a deep breath, the boy straightened his shoulders and put on his best brave face. And for a seven year-old boy who was more timid than outgoing, it was a bold move.

"I follow the edge of the bushes until there," he said and pointed to the bare apple tree. "No snow there, so no footprints."

"Good."

He continued to point his way to the front porch, his finger tracing a line in the foggy window of Quincy's mom's Honda. "Then I go under the windows to the front porch. But I don't walk on the porch, I reach through the rail and leave the bag on the welcome mat."

Quincy grinned and nodded at him. "You've got it. And what next?"

After another deep breath, Olly motioned to the house. "Then I ring the doorbell."

"That's right. How are you going to reach it?"

"I'm going to brush some of that snow off and lift myself up on the railing to reach the doorbell. Then jump back down and run."

"Noooo."

Olly's wide eyes fixed on Quincy. He trusted his mom's friend, but he wasn't sure about her plan. "Quincy, she's going to catch me if I don't run."

"No. Listen, bud. Look at her porch- it's full of snow. She's not going anywhere. She'll open the door, see the bag, lift it up and look around. Then she might wait a few minutes to see if anything is moving. She might call out, *Thank you*, or something, but she's not coming down those steps. Trust me. You just stay put, right there between those two bushes. And after the door closes, you count to..."

After a gulp, he finished her sentence. "I count to twenty, then I come back the way I came. And you'll be right here, right?"

"Yep. I'm not going to move a muscle. I promise."

"And she won't be mad?"

"Oh bud, she's going to be so happy. She's alone, Olly. This will be her first Christmas without her husband. She lives alone now and doesn't have anyone to even talk to tonight. She's going to feel so happy to have someone think of her."

Olly's shoulders relaxed. "Yeah. I want her to be happy."

"Right? And I know she loves molasses cookies. She's told my mom that they're her favorite, so you're going to make her happy. I promise."

"Okay."

"Are you ready?"

Quincy's heart just about exploded when she saw him swallow and nod. Such a brave little man!

"I'm ready."

Quincy turned off the lights in the car, so when he opened the door, nothing gave them away. Olly closed the door without letting it latch shut, then crouching down, he quickly followed the shoulder of the road down a hundred feet, then sprinted across the street and followed the shoulder back until he was in position. He adjusted his grip on the bright red and green gift bag in his sweaty palm and began his intrepidacious trip along the bushes edging her lawn.

"You've got this, bud," Quincy whispered to herself. She was so proud of him for being brave. She knew he wasn't a daring type of little boy; he had too much to worry about for a seven year-old. But doorbell ditching was her very favorite Christmas memory of her childhood and she wanted Olly to have this experience, too. She wished she could give him a better childhood, but her time and resources were limited. No, the Twelve Days of Christmas, doorbell ditching-style was the best she could do right now. And no one deserved twelve days of love more than Grandma Berty.

Under the apple tree, Olly clung to the trunk, twisting and turning to make sure no car was driving by, or random person was out walking their dog. But eight o'clock on a Thursday night, eleven days before Christmas, this semi-rural street was as quiet as he could hope for. Carefully avoiding the spotty patches of snow, Olly crept towards the house and reminded himself to keep under the windows all the way to the front porch.

It wasn't hard to brush a line of snow away from the edge of the cement and pull himself up by the railing. The bag was too fat to fit through the black metal rails, but it was easy to lift it over and drop it dead center of the welcome mat. He had to shuffle a little to the left to reach the doorbell and he glanced down, making sure he knew where he would land when he jumped after the dreaded ringing of the doorbell.

One deep breath. Then another, and he was ready to reach out and... The doorbell was much louder than he expected and it startled a squeak out of him. Olly jumped down and forgetting their getaway plan, sprinted across the snow to Quincy's car.

"Oh no," she moaned. Quincy prayed he'd get to the car before Grandma Berty got up from her recliner and to the door. But instead of jumping inside the car and slamming the door shut, as she feared he'd do, Olly raced beyond the car and hunkered down on the other side long before Grandma's door opened and the warm orange glow brightened her front porch.

The once-tall, elderly woman with thin grey hair, stood in the doorway and Quincy could hear her muffled exclamation as she discovered the gift bag. She couldn't see her clearly because the back window was so foggy, but she could hear her well with the door still cracked open.

"Oh! What is this? Do I have a secret santa? How exciting! Does my secret santa want to come in for some hot cocoa?"

After a long minute of silence, she chuckled. "Okay, well, it's an open invitation. Thank you! Merry Christmas!"

The door closed and after counting to twenty, Quincy sat up in her seat and peeked back at the house. She saw the front curtains flutter and she spoke loudly. "Stay where you are, Olly T. She's still watching out the window."

After another couple of minutes, the curtains had stilled and she felt it was safe for Olly to come out of hiding.

"C'mon out, bud. You did it!"

Olly's cheeks were flushed and his eyes were wide as he edged his way around the front of the car. "Did she see me?"

"Nope! You made it! Day one was a success!"

He pulled the door open and had to close the door three times before it latched properly. He was still afraid to make too much noise.

Pushing himself between the front seats, Olly whispered excitedly at Quincy. "And we get to do this tomorrow night, too?"

"Absolutely. We'll switch it up a little to keep her guessing. I'm coming to get you right after school tomorrow, so we can deliver it before I go to work."

"Wait. In the day? She'll see me!"

"Nope. We'll make a plan. You'll see. We can make it all twelve days, bud. And what happens if we make it all twelve days?"

Olly smiled his big smile. His rare smile. "Day After Christmas Surprise," he said.

"That's right. The Day After Christmas Surprise. If we get through all twelve days of Christmas without getting caught, on the day after Christmas, there is a fun surprise."

He giggled to himself and buckled his seatbelt.

Quincy pulled off the curb and drove down the lane before she flipped her lights back on. She glanced in the rearview mirror at little Olly T– Oliver Thomas– and fought back a few tears. Olly didn't need any tears from her. He needed joy. He needed a good memory to hopefully begin replacing the bad ones. And as a poor college student, home for the winter break, she didn't have a lot to give him, but she knew the power of Christmas service. It was a special kind of love. That, she could give him.

That Might Suck The Fun Out Of It

After dropping Olly at his mom's apartment, Quincy took the long way home and drove by her old high school. The lot was filled with cars– probably a basketball game, or maybe even a school production, but she wasn't interested in stopping by. The hard part about coming back to the hometown was not really fitting in anywhere, anymore. She was not looking forward to the long break away from her roommates and classes. She was lucky to have been assigned really great roommates and had built an active social life at school. It was going to be a long boring break with her brothers not coming home and no high school friends she really wanted to reconnect with.

Mom raised her eyebrows expectantly when Quincy walked into the kitchen. Quincy flashed her a smile and a thumbs up instead of explaining how it went because Mom had her phone pressed between her ear and her shoulder.

"Really? What was it?" Mom said, winking at Quincy. "No," she gasped. "Those are your favorite!"

After a long listening break, Mom chuckled. "Well, don't eat them all tonight! That much sugar will make you sick."

Quincy sat at the counter and chuckled, too.

"Quincy is hoping to stop by and see you this weekend. They started her working the same day she got home, so she hasn't had a lot of free time, but she'll be over after church on Sunday."

After another listening pause, Mom's eyebrows popped up. "Really? From Boston? Ohh, *Boston*. Well, Berty, that's wonderful news! I can't wait to meet your grandson. I'll talk to you soon. Goodnight!"

"A grandson? Did she say a grandson was coming?" Quincy groaned. "That could mess with our doorbell ditching." A grandson could get to the door a lot faster than an eighty-something widow with a bad hip. That's not good news for Olly.

Mom nodded to the plate of cookies on the counter. "Did you try one?"

"Not yet. I can't eat any sugar until the twentieth. I still have a few days left on my no-sugar challenge."

Mom shrugged and took a cookie for herself. Quincy's eyes followed the cookie to her mouth and she sighed.

"How did it go?" Mom asked.

"He was so stinking cute. I'm not even kidding. I want to keep him in my pocket."

Mom smiled. "He is the cutest. And he didn't get caught? Good for him!"

"It was closer than it should've been. He panicked and took off across the yard, making big old footprints across the snow."

Mom winced then laughed. "It's good for him. He'll be twice as sneaky tomorrow."

"I'll get him after school tomorrow and I'll keep him until I go to work. His mom should be home by then."

"Sounds good. See if he'll make gift tags, or maybe even help with one of the gifts."

"Yeah. Tags, for sure. But I don't know if I want him working on the gifts. I don't want him focusing on the gifts too much or it may dawn on him that we're doing the same gifts for him and his mom. If he gets that, it might suck the fun right out of it."

Mom pushed off from the counter and glanced at the clock. "Hmm. Well, gift tags, or notes, or something. Let him have a little skin in the game."

"All right. Hey, do you want to watch a movie or something with me tonight?"

"I work tomorrow. School isn't out, yet. One more day."

"Oh, sure. Sorry, Mom. Yeah, you'd better get to bed. Is Dad already asleep?"

"No. He isn't home, yet. He and Uncle Jed are working on the chair for Lindsay."

"That's cool. Okay. Well, I might, I don't know. I'm just going to..." She couldn't think of anything to do.

Mom hugged her and kissed her cheek. "Maybe you can work on the scarf."

"Yeah. I'll work on that. Thanks for reminding me. Okay. Goodnight, Mom."

After Mom left the kitchen, Quincy scowled at the plate of cookies. She'd worked hard the summer before she left for school and lost almost thirty pounds. She'd worked even harder to not gain the *freshman fifteen* pounds her first semester of college and now that she was home again, she knew it would be an uphill battle to keep the extra weight off with all of these baked goods and regular meals. She'd have to throw in some extra exercise if she was going to maintain her healthy weight.

She sighed and left the cookies behind, sinking into the old cushy couch in the family room where she had left the chunky red yarn and hook. She had already finished the smaller scarf for Olly and was now working on the bigger one for Grandma Berty. This was the gift for the tenth day. Her own grandmother had taught her to crochet when she was a little girl and she had plenty of practice. The scarves were going fast. Maybe she'd make one for Olly's mom, too.

Quincy wished her older brothers could have brought their families home this year, but both of them were with their wives' families for the holidays. It was only fair that they split the time between both sides. Besides, they both had cute new babies this past year and their adorable little kids were favorites wherever they went. She didn't begrudge her sisters-in-law time with their families. Not that much, anyway.

It took her a few minutes to choose a playlist and she settled into the couch. She picked up the deep red yard and her L hook, and with a great sigh, she picked up where she left off on Grandma Berty's scarf.

Higher Stakes

"Okay my friend, are you ready for this?"

Quincy parked down the road so Grandma Berty wouldn't recognize her mom's car in the daylight. But as they stood, hidden from view by the trunk of a towering blue spruce, Olly shook his head over and over.

"I'm going to get caught. There's no way I can get out of there in time." His eyes raked over the inch of new snow that accumulated during his last day of school and he shrunk back further behind the spruce branch.

Quincy took another look at the house and tried to see the situation through Olly's panicked eyes. Okay, the curtains were open, that was true, but she could see an easy exit off the porch to the right and around the house. They had discussed it, but he wasn't having any of it.

"I still think you'll be good if you hustle around the house and hide behind the corner until she goes back in."

Olly squinted at the front door and she watched his eyes make the path around the house. "Nope."

She couldn't help but laugh at his stubbornness. It reminded her a lot of herself when she first knocked a door under the watchful eyes of her daring big brothers. She took a step back and folded her arms over her chest. "Okay, little man. Let's come up with a plan B, then."

Olly folded his arms over his chest and stared back at her. "Come back after dark?"

"I have to work tonight. It has to be now. We can figure this out."

As Quincy and Olly stared at the tidy rancher through the branches, a silver SUV turned onto the lane. Quincy pulled Olly with her under the lowest branch and they huddled close to the prickly trunk.

Grandma Berty's garage door lumbered open on loud and squeaky tracks as the SUV pulled into her driveway. A woman from their congregation stepped down and cheerfully greeted Grandma and helped her into the vehicle. Olly grinned widely at Quincy when the SUV backed out of the driveway and sped down the road.

"Ha!" He offered her a high five and Quincy had to hold herself back from pulling the adorable second grader into a smothering hug. She settled for giving him a sharp high five.

As they walked the second gift bag to the front porch, Olly frowned at the tracks they were making in the white sheet of snow on the driveway. "Should we be walking in the tire tracks?"

Quincy glanced down, and then to the house. "I have a better idea." She nodded at a snow shovel standing near the garage door. "Let's clear her porch and steps, and..." She pointed to the walk and the driveway.

Olly's eyes followed Quincy's finger. "We could clear the whole thing and we wouldn't have any tracks for anything we drop off until it snows again!"

She nodded. "And bonus: it would make it much safer for her if she wanted to walk to her mailbox," she said, pointing back to the street.

Olly's eyes widened and he nodded. "We should clear it all."

"Okay, Olly T, let's go fast. We don't know how long she'll be gone. Why don't you set the bag on her porch now. That way, if we have to run and hide, it will already be in place."

Olly ran the gift bag to the welcome mat and then ran back to the snow shovel before Quincy could get to it. Quincy talked him through shoveling the driveway, walk, and he let her help on the steps. He made double sure the second gift was secure before they set the shovel back against the garage.

Olly broke out into skipping on the way back to the car, taking Quincy's hand and swinging it between them. Quincy felt like her heart was glowing. She squeezed his hand and skipped with him.

Plan A

Saturday night was a problem. When Quincy and Olly drove by Grandma Berty's house, the curtains stood wide open and there were people walking around in the front room. The gift bag tonight was large and cumbersome and not easily dropped. The chances of being seen were high with the curtains open and someone moving around in the front room.

"What should we do?" Olly slid down in his seat when a man walked in front of the window.

"It's okay, Olly, we have options. A: we can divide and conquer. I run around back and knock on the door and distract them, then you drop the package and ring the doorbell and run. B: we can get the package up on the porch on the blind side, then use a long stick to ring the doorbell so we won't waste time coming down the stairs. Or C..." Quincy took a deep breath and blew it out. "One of us will drop the package and the other one will ring the bell and dive into the bush and stay very still until they go back inside."

Olly stared at Quincy with wide eyes and a dropped jaw. He was in awe of her audacity. He gulped and looked back to the house.

"Plan A. How will I know when you've knocked on the back door?" Olly whispered.

Quincy rolled her shoulders. "After you're in place by the porch, I'll walk around back." She drew a deep breath. "I'll whoop really loud- the whole neighborhood will hear me. Then I'll knock loudly on the door. You'll count to five... one alligator, two alligator, and then ring the doorbell and run to the big tree. Stay on the other side of the trunk until I come get you."

"What if they find me?"

"They won't. If they start in your direction, I'll distract them and run down the road in the opposite direction and they'll try to follow me."

Olly stared at the house and nodded over and over. "Okay."

"Okay. We've got this Olly T. It's worth it. She's going to love this one."

Olly grinned. He knew this would be Grandma Berty's favorite. They had spent hours painting a Nativity set of ceramic figures. They brushed them with dark shoe polish and then rubbed them off using old towels. They finished the figurines in a dusty brown color that looked antique when they were done polishing them. They had made two sets and since Quincy's family already had a Nativity, Olly would take the second set home. He was so excited to present the Nativity to his mother.

"Let's do this. Do you know how to army crawl?"

As they circled the property to get to the driveway, they discussed the finer points of army crawling. After Olly crawled under the windows and was firmly in place on the front porch, Quincy left him and made her way to the back door.

She knew the property well; she had spent plenty of time doing yard work for Grandma Berty and Grandpa Doug, and had been in their house a hundred times. She knew how long it would take them to walk from the front room to the back door. She would even be able to see the top of the head of whomever answered the door through a high window before they reached the door.

Quincy slid into place and peeked through the back window. She could see Grandma sitting in her recliner, talking animatedly to a man with short brown hair. She tried to think of a way to yell loudly that wouldn't alarm Grandma too much and still be loud enough to signal to Olly to ring the doorbell. She decided on a Tarzan yell and giggled to herself. This was going to take a big breath.

The moment before Quincy was going to call, however, a wave of mortification hit her. *What was she doing?* She was nineteen years old, hiding in the cold in the back yard of an elderly woman, in the middle of December, about to yell like Tarzan. Why in the world was she doing this?

She took a deep breath and thought of little Olly Thomas, ready on the front porch. She thought how horrible his last year had been after his father left, leaving his mother to find a job at a local grocery store so they could survive out of the homeless shelter they'd spent a month in. How he came home from school every day to his cranky aged great aunt, who watched over him until his mother returned from work. How traumatizing it must've been, when he came home his first day back to school after Thanksgiving, to find his great aunt lying unresponsive on the couch.

Now that he was alone in the apartment, kind people in their congregation had been helping out to keep him safe after school until his mother was off work. And paperwork was being processed for an after-school program that would start after the holidays. But poor Olly had lived through years of neglect and emotional abuse, then abandonment, and now loss. He could really use some joy in his young life. A little excitement. A lot of love.

And this was all in fun, she reminded herself. After all, Grandma Berty would eventually know who all these gifts came from and they would laugh about it all in a few days. Quincy could handle a little mortification to bring some joy into Olly's life. And Grandma Berty's. Quincy would be happy to.

That thought was enough to overcome her momentary mortification, and after taking a deep breath, Quincy yelled the loudest Tarzan call she could yell. She even beat her chest to make it sound right.

Ouch. That hurt.

Then she knocked loudly on the back door. Ouch. That hurt, too! And when she saw the top of the man's head almost to the door, she took off, deeper into the back yard, and turned a quick corner, flattening herself to the back side of a tool shed.

She heard the door open before she hit the tool shed, and sweated out the next seven seconds.

"Hello? Hey! Who's out there? I can see—"

She heard the familiar chimes of the doorbell echo through the house and then the back door slammed shut.

Quincy peeked around the shed, then ran to the front yard like the devil was after her. She flattened herself against the house and tried to calm her breathing.

The man was now on the front porch. He bent down to pick up the bright green gift bag and chuckled. "Grandma, you have a present."

"Oh! I forgot about my secret santa! Are they still there? Thank you!"

The man smirked. "Thanks, Tarzan!"

She heard Olly's giggle from the blue spruce and winced when the man's head turned toward the sound, as well. Quincy breathed a sigh of relief when he brought the gift inside and shut the door. Then she waited. And waited. And waited.

Something told her that they were still at the window, watching. She called in a loud whisper, "Don't move a muscle, buddy. Just hang on."

After several minutes, the light reflecting on the snow-covered front lawn changed. The friendly orange glow shrunk until the curtains were completely drawn closed, and only then did Quincy brave walking straight to the road, crossing the street, and jogging past the house and then crossing back to the blue spruce.

Olly ran out and almost tackled her in a hug. "We did it! Did you see that guy? Did you see him? That was awesome!"

Quincy held his hand and they walked down the road to her dad's truck, Olly reliving each moment of tonight's gift drop in detail.

Basketball With A Stranger

After returning Olly to his mom, Quincy felt jittery. Restless. Bored. Her parents were out with some friends and she could not bring herself to go home and crochet another scarf. But what to do?

There was nothing to do in this town! Well, nothing to do alone, anyway. She had let her gym membership lapse when she left for college and couldn't afford to start it all back up just for the winter break. What would she do if her brothers were here?

They'd go to the church and play basketball in the multi-purpose room. "You know what? Why not?" she murmured to herself. She could shoot hoops for an hour or so and burn off this steam. A quick text to her mom resulted in the digital key code to the church building and she was on her way. She knew where the basketballs were stored.

At the church, Quincy connected to the sound system and started one of her workout playlists. She dribbled the ball back and forth and shot from every spot she could think of. She went through a few drills she remembered from high school ball and had worked up a good sweat by the time her mom texted asking her to open the door for Grandma Berty's grandson.

She dialed her mother immediately. "What? Why? What is he doing here?"

Her mom laughed. "He's bored. He wants to play basketball."

She heard someone knocking at the front doors and startled. "Mom! Are you serious?"

"Oh stop. It's just a kid who's bored. Let him in and share the gym, you big baby."

"Mom," she moaned. "You don't get it."

Another knock.

"Do it," Mom said and ended the call.

Quincy held the basketball to her hip and made her way to the foyer. She could see him through the glass door. She didn't recognize him until he turned to look back at the parking lot. She recognized his short brown hair.

It took her twenty seconds to fix her long brown ponytail and straighten her college gym t-shirt over her messy sweats. The young man turned back to the door and his face lit up when he saw her through the glass. Quincy pretended that his smile didn't start her heart pumping faster. She pushed the door open with a good shove and nodded for him to come in.

"Thanks! Are you sure you don't mind if I hang out? My grandma is already in bed and it's only eight o'clock."

"Yeah. It's no problem. I'm just wasting time; I'm not a baller or anything."

He laughed. "You're not a baller? What does that mean? You're holding a ball, so you're a baller."

She chuckled and shook her head. "I'm just messing around. I haven't played basketball since high school."

The boy shrugged. "I'm not an athlete. I'm more of a mathlete," he joked. "I only exercise so I can justify how much candy I eat."

Quincy spit out a laugh and led the way back to the gym.

"And when I'm incredibly bored," he added, beckoning to her to pass him the ball. "Want to see me not make a basket?" The young man slowly dribbled the ball to the free throw line and tossed the ball towards the hoop with two hands and bent elbows. It barely grazed the rim. "See?"

Quincy chuckled and picked up another ball. "Okay, so how about we just shoot? Pick a spot and shoot. If you make it there, I'll stand there and shoot from the same spot."

"What if I don't make it?" he asked, picking up another ball from the floor.

"Then I'll shoot from a spot and you try it."

"Let me clarify," he said. "How am I going to lose this game?"

She laughed and shook her head. "We're just shooting. There doesn't have to be a winner. We're just wasting time, right?"

"Yep. It's either that or I hunt down the little kids ding dong ditching my grandma."

"What?"

He laughed and dribbled a few times before he shot. "Yeah. It was cute. A bunch of little kids are dropping cookies and stuff on her porch. They ring the doorbell, then run."

"Oh yeah? That is cute."

"Yeah. I'm going to catch them tomorrow," he said, bouncing a ball to her.

"How do you know they're coming back?" She sank another ball and glanced at him before she chased her ball down.

"I don't," he said. "But I'll bet they will. My guess is they're going to count down to Christmas." He laughed and turned to her. "Hey, what's your name? I'm Boston."

She tilted her head and blinked. "You're from Boston?"

He smirked. "No. I'm from Nevada. My name is Boston."

"Oh! Cool. I'm Quincy," she said, holding the ball on her hip. She was not prepared for him to roll his eyes and grumble when she told him her name. "What?"

"Ha. Ha." He picked up another ball and shot, this time hitting the backboard and almost making it in the hoop.

"Wait. Why do you say it like that?"

He glanced at her, then stared harder. "Your name is Quincy? Serious?"

"Yes."

He narrowed his eyes and stepped wider. "Your name is Quincy? Like Quincy, Massachusetts?"

"I don't know if there's a Quincy in Massachusetts. I know there's a Quincy in Illinois. And one here in Washington."

A slow smile spread across his face and Quincy's breath caught. It was a dazzling sort of smile.

"I thought you were messing with me. People do that all of the time because of Boston, Massachusetts."

"Oh. Ohhh, sure. I get it. Ha. Nope. I'm just Quincy. My friends call me Quin sometimes if you like that better," she said then took a shot and missed by a mile.

"Quincy is a great name. It's called the City of Presidents. A bunch of former presidents were born there, or lived there."

"Have you been there?"

"Yes. So, my dad used to teach at Harvard. We lived in Massachusetts until I was in high school."

"Dang. That's cool. Why did he leave Harvard?"

"He took a job at UNLV as a department head. That and my mom was sick of winters."

"Ah. Yeah, snow can be a downer."

They moved into a pattern of one person shooting while the other rebounded the ball, then switching every few minutes. They didn't talk about it; it just happened as they talked.

Boston explained that he had just flown in that afternoon to stay with his grandma for a little while. Quincy explained how her brothers weren't home and she didn't want to go back to her high school friends. She didn't feel that they were moving in the same direction. Boston explained how he had been abroad the last two years and would be starting college in January, and he was concerned that he wouldn't be able to handle roommates. Quincy told him about her roommates and some of the fun things they had done together.

It was easy conversation, and before they knew it, it was ten o'clock and Quincy's mom texted to remind her to get to bed in time to wake up for early church services in the morning.

They gathered up the balls and stashed them back in the closet before they locked the door on their way out.

"So, do you know my grandma?" Boston asked on their way out.

"Yes. She and my mom are good friends. We attend the same congregation."

"Oh! That's cool. So, I'll see you at church tomorrow?"

She smiled at him and nodded. "I told her I was coming to visit tomorrow afternoon." She cleared her throat nervously. "I don't have to. I didn't know she had family in town..."

Boston walked her to her dad's truck. "You should come. We could play a game with Grandma. She loves that stuff."

"Okay. That would be cool. Well, it was nice to meet you, Boston. I guess I'll see you tomorrow."

"You too, Quincy. See you in the morning." He tapped her hood twice before he walked to his grandma's old Buick.

She waited to make sure his car started after it sputtered in the cold, and they waved one last time before she pulled out to the right and he pulled to the left.

Boston couldn't hear Quincy giggling to herself about the boy with short brown hair and pretty blue eyes who couldn't make a basket to save his life.

And Quincy didn't see Boston thump the steering wheel and mutter, "Sweet!" because he was now excited to take his grandma to church in the morning and see the pretty girl with a perfect smile who put him instantly at ease.

Someone To Hang Out With

On Sunday afternoon, Quincy and Olly brought a warm loaf of bread, fresh from the oven, to Grandma Berty, and pretended to pick up a gift bag that had been on the doorstep when they arrived. Quincy said she'd seen a red car. Olly giggled and said it was going really fast.

Grandma played *Go Fish* with them until she needed a nap. Quincy offered to take Boston and Olly to see a musical light show in a neighboring street while Grandma rested. They sat through the musical performance twice then found a few more streets with amazing light displays before she had to get Olly home to his mom.

Driving back to Grandma Berty's house, Boston asked what plans she had for winter break and she explained that she was working at her high school waitressing job to get some money stashed away for the next semester.

"I'm on scholarship, so that pays for tuition and books. My parents pay my housing, so if I can save up enough for groceries, I won't have to work next semester. It's worth it to work while I'm home and not doing anything else, so I can have more free time when I'm back with people I want to hang out with."

Boston flinched. Quincy flushed. "That didn't come out right," Quincy murmured.

Boston coughed a laugh.

Quincy cleared her throat and hoped he didn't notice her red cheeks. "I mean, generally-speaking. It's worth it for me to take shifts at the restaurant during my break so I don't have to work during the semester. That's what I meant."

Boston nodded silently.

"I didn't know I'd meet someone I actually wanted to hang out with," she said, then blushed even more red. "I mean..."

Boston smiled at her. "So. Are you willing to do something besides basketball after work tomorrow?"

"I close tomorrow. I'm not done until nine."

Boston shrugged. "A movie? I could come to your house. A game? Just not *Go Fish*, please."

Quincy chuckled. "*Go Fish* is the best."

Boston snorted and rolled his eyes. "A movie. I'll bring candy."

She shook her head. "I can't eat candy for a few more days."

"A few more days?"

After a moment of deliberation, Quincy explained how she had worked hard to become more healthy and was trying to not eat processed sugar.

Boston frowned. "That's amazing. Very amazing, but...." He shook his head. "I can't live without sugar. And it wars with every fiber of my being to watch a movie without movie candy."

She pulled into his grandma's driveway and laughed. "I didn't say you couldn't eat candy; I said I wouldn't eat candy."

"Popcorn?"

"Absolutely."

"Soda pop?" he asked.

"Sugar-free," she countered.

"Caffeinated or no?"

He looked so serious, it was hard to not laugh at him.

"Umm. Either. But what I really like are those flavored sparkling waters."

Boston nodded. "Okay. I can handle the snacks. You pick a movie and I'll be over about nine-thirty. Does that sound all right?"

"Sounds good. Do you want me to text you my address?"

"Yes." He pulled out his phone and looked up when he was ready to add her number. "Okay, let's have it."

She told him her number and he immediately texted her so she had his.

"Thanks for the light show," Boston said, glancing at the front door. "I guess I'd better get back to Grandma."

"Yeah. Thanks for coming along. I'll see you tomorrow."

Boston smiled his dazzling smile again. "I'll see you tomorrow." He held up his phone. "But you can text me anytime."

Quincy blushed and tried to hold back a giggle. "You too, Boston."

"Goodnight, Quincy," he sang and pushed himself out of her car. "Drive safe."

"Goodnight."

And Quincy couldn't see Boston rock his eyebrows as he walked to his grandma's porch. "A movie," he murmured happily.

And Boston didn't hear Quincy giggle when she remembered how he sang her name.

Sharing The Love

"I need to get Olly over there early this morning so Boston doesn't get suspicious of me," she explained to Mom over breakfast Monday morning. "That way if he brings it up, I can tell him that it couldn't have been me because I was at work."

Mom shook her head. "But you won't be at work this morning, and he knows that."

"No, see, that's why it's genius," Quincy said. "See, he'll say, *But you weren't at work*. And I'll say, *Yes, I was. I left by noon and didn't get off until after eight*. And then he'll say, *but it was delivered in the morning*, then I'll be all.... *Ohhh. It came in the morning? Well, you didn't mention that. Sure, it could've been me*. And I'll laugh and say something like, *I bake stuff every night, kind of like a kitchen elf. Remind me, what did I bake last night?* And it isn't a baked good, so he'll doubt. I'll totally gas-light him."

Mom laughed and shook her head. "It could go that way," she said. And after the last bite of her scrambled eggs she said, "But it might not. That conversation could go very differently."

"Hmm."

"But what if it was delivered while you and he were cuddled up, watching a movie?"

"Mom!" Quincy choked on her sip of grape juice and barely got a napkin to her mouth in time to control the spray. "You did not just say that! We are not going to be cuddling! Oh my gosh, you're traumatizing."

Mom snickered and wiggled her eyebrows.

"Besides, it would be too obvious if you or Dad were gone while he was here. He would know that one of you did it."

"Stephanie could do it," Mom said. "She'll be off work by then. The roads are good, her tires can handle it. Let Olly and his mom do this one. Stephanie could use a little giggle, too."

Quincy had to think about it. She felt jealous; she wanted the time with Olly. Not to mention, she craved the fun of it. But Mom was probably right.

"Besides, it will be the easiest night for them to do it," Mom said, taking her dishes to the sink. "Better let them have tonight. Boston may redouble his efforts tomorrow."

Complication

Mom was right. Monday night was a breeze. Olly and his mom had no trouble delivering the large basket of interesting and exotic fruit while Boston and Quincy laughed with Mom and Dad over a classic comedy that Boston had never seen.

But Tuesday was a problem.

BOS: grandma is having some of her friends over tonight to play bunco

BOS: do you want to come over and help me out?

QUI: what do you need help with?

QUI: I'm pretty sure you have enough charisma to charm a room full of grandmas all by yourself

BOS: thanks?

BOS: I'm going to catch the ding dong ditcher tonight

BOS: grandma wants to know who it is so she can thank them

QUI: she should let them finish and catch them on Christmas

BOS: we won't be here for Christmas

QUI: what??

BOS: I thought you knew that

BOS: sorry!

Quincy sat back in her seat and frowned out the front windshield. She was due to start work in ten minutes and was waiting with her mom for a few minutes before she had to go in.

Mom touched her arm. "Quin? What's wrong?"

"Did you know that Grandma Berty won't be here for Christmas?"

"What? Yes, she will."

Quincy showed her mom the texts.

"Ask him why," Mom said. Her brows furrowed and now she frowned out the front windshield, too.

QUI: where is she going?

BOS: can you talk?

QUI: for about 3 minutes

Her phone vibrated in her hand and she glanced at Mom. Neither of them smiled.

"Hey, Boston."

"Hey! Are you heading in to work?"

"Yep. So, tell me her cool Christmas plans."

Boston cleared his throat. "Well. It's why I'm here. I have to help Grandma decide what she's bringing with her."

"What do you mean? Bringing with her where?"

Boston was silent for a moment. "Grandma's moving to Nevada. Dad wants her closer to him. He found a really cool place in a retirement community close to us."

Mom gasped and slapped a hand over her mouth. Quincy was at a complete loss for words.

"Does she know?" Mom whispered.

Quincy cleared her throat and had to do it twice to be able to choke out words. "Does she know she's leaving?"

Boston sighed. "Dad is going to tell her on Friday, when he gets here."

"Friday, huh? Then you leave Saturday?"

"Yeah." Boston's voice was sad. Quincy and Mom could both hear it.

It took Quincy a minute to speak. "Wow. That sucks."

"It will be better for Grandma. Dad can't take care of her here, and ..."

"And what?"

Boston sighed. "We can't take care of my mom in Vegas and Grandma in Washington. It's too much. We need them in the same place."

Quincy desperately wanted to ask Boston why they had to take care of his mom, but she was due to start work in about sixty seconds. "Okay. So, I would love to come over tonight, but I can't come until after work. But I have a lunch break around four-thirty if you want to bring Grandma by for dinner."

"Cool. I'll ask if she'll do it. She doesn't let me take her out that much."

"Either way is good. It's no problem. Listen, I have to go. We'll talk more later, k?"

"Yeah. Thanks, Quincy. I'm sorry I didn't tell you sooner. I feel bad."

"It's fine, Boston. I have to go. Bye."

Quincy ended the call and grabbed her bag and rushed from the car to the restaurant, brushing away tears before she pulled the door open to start one of the longest shifts of her life.

Boston didn't show up on her lunch break and it was probably better that way. Quincy found an empty table in the back, and sat alone, watching her phone for a message that never came.

She looked up UNLV, and traced the route from her college to his. Over five hours driving time. She looked up airline tickets and was pleasantly surprised to see that it was only thirty-eight dollars for a round trip ticket on a sale in February. She set a travel alert to notify her when sales between their two college cities came up, then she slid her phone into her pocket and asked herself why she was looking up how far it was to his college.

And Boston couldn't see her wipe a tear away at the frustration of losing him before she had a chance to see what might develop between them. And Quincy couldn't see that Boston had been scouring the internet for travel routes and airplane tickets, as well. She had no way of knowing that Boston was determined to pursue a friendship with Quincy whether he left before Christmas or not.

A Tough One

"Okay, Olly. This is going to be a tough one, but I think we can do it."

Olly's eyes gleamed and he nodded his head vigorously. "We can do a distraction again, but this time actually leave the gift on the back porch."

Quincy blinked at him. "You're a genius, Olly T. A genius." She sniffed and peeked through the spruce branches. "Do you want to do the front or back door this time?"

"Back."

Of course. She was going to have to be the decoy again. Oof. "Okay, do you want to go scope it out, so you know where to hide, just in case?"

Olly nodded and so they snuck around to the back and plotted their escape routes. A thought struck her just as she was about to leave him to get into position at the front door. "You're going to have to yell really loud, Olly. Like, *really loud*. Can you do a Tarzan yell?"

He froze and blinked at her. "No. I can't do a Tarzan yell."

"What can you do?"

After a moment's deliberation, he rolled his shoulders back and lifted his chin. "I can do a really loud HO HO HO."

Quincy smiled widely and patted his back. "You're a rockstar, Olly T. A freaking rockstar. Let's do this."

As Quincy rounded the house to place the gift bag on the front steps, she heard Olly start his loud HO HO HO and she froze. It was too early!

But when the front door was flung open wide and Boston flew out to the front porch, she was instantly grateful she hadn't had time to get to the front steps. Boston saw through their ruse!

"I know you're out there," Boston called. "Where are you, little santa? Come out, come out, wherever you are!"

She heard Boston's slow steps down the front porch and her heart stopped. *Don't turn left, don't turn left.*

He turned left.

Quincy flattened herself against the side of the house and slid down to the ground. *Oh no.*

Then Olly's little voice rang out again, "HO HO HO! Merry Christmas!" from the back yard and the next thing she knew, Boston was flying past her, on his way to the back yard.

Without stopping to think, Quincy popped up and sprinted to the front porch, sending the gift bag flying through the open door and into the front room. She continued to sprint across the driveway and down the street until she realized that she needed to meet Olly back under the blue spruce. As she slowly crept back towards Grandma's house, however, she saw movement under the towering spruce that was too tall to be Olly.

"Where are you, you sneaky little sneaker?" Boston muttered, chuckling to himself. "I know this is where you hide out."

Quincy dropped to the ground once again. This time she was hidden behind a low boulder planted along the side of the road to discourage people from parking in front of Grandma's neighbor's house.

She stayed still and silent, with her eyes on the trunk of the spruce, waiting for Boston to leave. But Boston stayed under the tree, even when Grandma Berty appeared at the door and laughed, calling out, "Boston! Here's the bag, honey! They already got away!"

He stayed hidden close to the trunk of the tree even then and it worried her. Olly was going to meet her under that spruce any minute unless he had seen Boston make it under the tree to hide. And she had no way of knowing if Olly saw him, or where he even was.

"You may be faster than me, and maybe even smarter, but I'm more patient," Boston murmured.

After a long ten minutes, Quincy was about to give herself up for worry that Olly was somewhere melting down, but then she heard a loud and merry, "HO HO HO! Merry Christmas!" from the back yard and Boston burst out from under the spruce and sprinted to the back yard.

Seconds later, Olly dashed to her from the other side of the house, shimmying through a narrow gap in a hedge. She stood up and waved at him, then started jogging towards the car. As soon as Olly caught up, they continued to run down the street and around the corner where Quincy had parked her mom's car.

"Olly, I'm in awe of you. You're a beast!" She offered him a high five and he hugged her instead.

"What's tomorrow, Quincy? Is it something light? I have an idea." He bounced up and down and hugged her again.

Cheering For The Doorbell Ditchers

When Quincy returned an hour later to hang out with Boston, it was with mixed emotions. Boston opened the door so quickly after she knocked, she stepped back in surprise.

Boston laughed. "Hey! It's you! I thought maybe they were coming twice in one night."

"I missed them?" She smiled. "Good. I'm cheering for the doorbell ditchers."

Boston smirked and ushered her in. Grandma Berty and a few of her friends were seated around her dining room table, chatting over a hand of cards. After greeting the ladies, Boston motioned for her to follow him down the hall to one of the back rooms. He stopped at Grandma's craft room and turned in. "Check this out."

Boston pointed to the craft table where there were a variety of home-sewn Christmas-themed pillowcases folded and stacked neatly. Next to the pillow cases sat several miniature Christmas stockings made from scraps of the same fabric. The stockings were filled to bursting with candies and had a candy cane hanging jauntily from the side.

"These are for when we catch them," he said, grinning. "Grandma has kept me busy."

Quincy fingered the stockings and smiled. It was definitely Grandma Berty's MO... A newly widowed woman in her eighties gets doorbell-ditched a few Christmas goodies and the first thing she does is try to give back. She was one of the most charitable people Quincy knew. Instead of dwelling on her own sadness, she looked for opportunities to bless the lives of others. And it was tearing her up inside that they were going to lose her to Nevada.

"There are five stockings. How many doorbell ditchers are there?"

Boston settled on the floor, leaning against the wall, and motioned for Quincy to take the only chair. Instead, Quincy settled on the floor across from him and tapped his knee with her toes. He grinned and moved to sit next to her against her wall.

"Well, I know there's at least two. And I suspect there are actually four. Maybe parents and three little kids. Fast little kids," he muttered, laughing at himself. "Either that or one little kid and a couple of teenagers."

Hmm. He was getting closer.

"I thought it was you for a while," Boston said, tapping her knee. "But I saw the getaway car once and it wasn't any of yours. Besides, you have an alibi for a couple of the deliveries."

"That's too bad," Quincy teased. "Because I like the red pillowcase."

Boston tapped her knee again and Quincy caught his finger with hers. After a few seconds, she let him go, but instead of pulling his hand back, he took hers in both of his and started tracing her fingers. Quincy leaned against his shoulder.

"Does she know, yet?" Quincy whispered.

Boston shook his head. "I know it's going to be hard. She's lived here for a long time and she's really loved here..."

Quincy nodded, but couldn't meet his eyes.

"But she's ours to take care of, you know? And we can't do it from three states away."

She nodded again.

"I'm sorry," he whispered. "She's told me about your family. You guys do a lot to take care of her. I know it will be hard for her to leave you."

"I'm going to miss her, but I know it's for the best. You know, she'll actually be closer to my college than my hometown when she's with you guys. Maybe I could visit her."

"Yeah. You know, our schools aren't that far apart. It's less than forty dollars to fly, and you could drive round trip on one tank of gas probably."

"I don't have a car at school," she whispered.

"I do," he said and squeezed her hand. "I could show you Vegas."

"That sounds cool. I've never been."

"You should come down and I'll show you my world."

Quincy grinned. "I'd like that."

They were quiet for several minutes. Boston smoothed his thumb down the side of her hand over and over.

"Is your mom okay?" she finally asked.

Boston took a deep breath and blew it out. "Mom is being treated for liver damage. Hepatitis. Cirrhosis."

"Oh, wow. I don't know that much about it, but it doesn't sound good."

He shook his head. "Nope. Not good."

"I'm sorry, Boston. What a hard Christmas this is for you."

Boston nodded, then smiled at her. "It's been better than I thought it would be."

Quincy met his eyes and smiled back at him. "Right? What are we going to do tonight? I don't have to be home until midnight. Should we play basketball again?"

Boston moaned and shook his head. "I can't play basketball to save my life, Quin. I'm serious."

He called her Quin! He totally used a nickname for her! Quincy's heart beat a little faster but she remained calm outwardly. Instead, she squeezed his hand. "How about volleyball?"

He groaned. "Chess?"

"Bowling?"

"A board game?"

"A board game after a walk?"

"I can do that," he said and squeezed her hand. "Where should we walk to? How about we go to a store and walk down the candy aisle?"

Quincy pretended to weep into her hands and Boston laughed. "Oh, no crying. Crying is for sissies. C'mon, Quin. Let's take a walk to find candy. And fruit. For you."

Boston took her hand to lead her to the kitchen, where they stopped to let Grandma Berty know that they would be gone for a few minutes. He didn't let go of her hand in front of his grandmother and her friends, which didn't seem like a big deal to him, but Quincy felt it keenly. Especially when a couple of Grandma's friends raised their eyebrows after glancing significantly at Quincy and Boston's hands.

Most of the ladies attended her family's congregation and it was obvious to Quincy that she would be a matter of gossip the second they walked out the front door.

And she wasn't wrong. But she didn't care.

A Whole Lot Of Dental Floss

Quincy had to move some of the gift deliveries around so they could still doorbell ditch the bigger items before Grandma had to leave on Saturday. After work, she was going to pick up Olly and they would wrap the scarves she had finished.

As far as Olly was concerned, it took her several tries to come up with the right size of scarves, and she had two extras. He agreed that one was just the right size for him, and another one would work really well for his mom. The other two ended up the perfect sizes for Grandma Berty and Boston. Olly was ready to deliver them with his very-involved plan that included a portable Bluetooth speaker and a whole lot of dental floss.

It took a few tries to release enough floss to toss the tightly-secured gift bag holding two red scarves up onto the roof and over the roof peak, but it was finally on the down slope. Olly kept a good hold of the small white container of dental floss as he crouched behind the house, below the dark laundry room window.

Quincy snuck back around to the front of the house and across the road to crouch behind the neighbor's pickup truck. She watched the gift bag slowly inch down the roof, past the chimney, until it fell off the side of the rain gutter and began swinging out and in and out over the front porch. She pulled her whistle out and got ready to blow it when the bag was about face-level to the front door.

One quick hard blow and the bag stopped moving. She waited to make sure the whistle hadn't raised a suspicious neighbor or doorbell ditch-ee, but no curtains moved and the door stayed shut. It was her turn now. She double checked that her portable speaker was paired with her phone then chose the doorbell ringtone and tapped PLAY.

Loud doorbell chimes echoed through the neighborhood from her speaker. She tapped it again, and again. Chills ran down her spine when she realized how many people could hear the doorbell echoing down the empty street. But no one came to their door except Boston and Grandma Berty, who looked around curiously.

Boston stared straight ahead at the brightly colored gift bag dangling in front of his face and Grandma howled with laughter when she saw it.

"Oh, Boston! They got us again!" She giggled and patted Boston's back. "Maybe tomorrow night, hon."

Boston smirked at the bag and gave it a tug. He kept pulling and pulling until the floss container dropped onto the porch in front of him. The look on his face was priceless and Quincy had to cover her mouth with both hands to smother the sound of her laughter.

"It's cheating if you don't ring the doorbell," he called out.

Quincy couldn't help herself and tapped her phone, and the doorbell chimed through the neighborhood again. Grandma laughed out loud and went inside to sit down, wiping her eyes.

Boston shook his head and chuckled. "Good one."

It's Going To Be Okay

Mom invited Grandma Berty and Boston to eat dinner with them on Wednesday and so Stephanie and Olly delivered the secret santa gift without incident, but Boston had a plan for Thursday which could be a problem.

"I need your help tonight," he said as soon as she came through the door of Grandma's house after work.

Quincy ignored him and went to hug Grandma Berty.

When she turned back to Boston, he had an odd look on his face.

"What?"

"Do I get a hug too, or do you only hug cute grandmas on Thursdays?"

"I hug cute grandmas and men named after cities in Massachusetts on Thursdays," Quincy replied, holding out her arms.

Boston scooped her up in a tight hug. "What a coincidence! I only hug girls named after cities in Massachusetts on Thursdays, too." He let her go then cleared his throat. "And grandmas," he amended and hugged his grandma, who patted his cheek and giggled before she shuffled down the hall.

"Will you help me catch the doorbell ditchers?" he whispered. "I want Grandma to get to meet them before my dad comes tomorrow."

There was already a plan in place to get the gift delivered tonight, but Quincy played along so Boston wouldn't guess.

"Oh. That's a good idea. I'll help you if you'll play basketball with me first." As soon as she got him away from the house, Stephanie and Olly would ditch the rest of the days' gifts in one big gift bag to Grandma. All except the last one. They would bring the last one tomorrow and wait on the porch for Grandma to answer. Olly was very excited to reveal himself.

But Boston shook his head. "I don't know when they're coming. We can't leave the house."

"I need to get some exercise in, Boston. Come up with something we can do while we're waiting for your secret santas."

"Why do you need to exercise? You're perfect just the way you are. You don't need to lose weight."

"Exercise is about being healthy. I'm on a roll; don't throw off my groove."

He spit out a laugh. "Don't throw off your groove, huh?"

"That's right. Don't throw off my groove. C'mon, let's go for a walk. Oh! We should doorbell ditch someone! Grab a few of the stockings." She turned to the hall. "Grandma Berty? Who should we doorbell ditch?"

Grandma came back into the room holding three stockings and a wide smile. "Olly Thomas, Kaylee and Henry Adams."

"Ooh. Perfect! We'll take these first; we can walk to the Adams's." She turned to Boston. "Let's go. Do you have a coat?"

He shook his head. "I had no time to pack. The best I have is a hoodie."

"No problem. We'll walk fast."

He rolled his eyes but didn't complain, and after pulling a UNLV hoodie over his head and wrapping a red scarf around his neck, he followed Quincy out the door.

Once they were on the road, Boston took her hand and chuckled. "I'm twenty-one," he said. "And you're the first girl I've held hands with. Is that weird or what?"

"I don't believe you."

"It's true. And I'm still surprised that you didn't like, drop my hand or tell me to knock it off."

Quincy stopped to gape at him. "Why would I do that?"

He shrugged. "You're really pretty. I'm sure you've had, I don't know..."

"Regrets? Yes. I've had regrets," she said and continued walking. "The people I hung out with in high school? They weren't my people. I made a lot of choices I regret trying to fit in here. We moved into this house my junior year. I went to school in another district before that. It was different there. A different culture."

"Like, more races were represented?"

"Not so much. It was just different. I have different ideas of family, and work, and humor."

Boston nodded. "Sense of humor, huh? So... am I funny?"

He grinned when she giggled. "I think you're funny," she assured him. "And I like how you treat your grandma."

He nodded and they walked in silence for a while. When Boston started talking, he was quiet. "I like how you treat people, too." He cleared his throat. "The first night I was here, I almost had a panic attack. I was kind of flown here last minute. My dad had a lot to handle at home and Grandma was calling and crying and it was just..." He shrugged. "So, I hopped on a plane the day after I got back from England."

"The day after you got home from England? Are you serious?"

Boston nodded. "I got home and everything was a mess. Dad was barely making it and couldn't handle Grandma being so sad. So I flew here in a hurry, and then everything came to a sudden halt. Grandma is the sweetest thing in the entire world, but she went to bed at like, seven-thirty. I had been busy for two years solid and suddenly I was stuck at Grandma's house a week before Christmas and I was supposed to figure out how to tell her that she had to leave her home... and I had no idea how to do that, or what to say, or anything. And there was no one to talk to about it. I just sat there, staring at the wall, freaking out." He shrugged. "I've never had that happen before. It was crazy."

"So, what made you think, *Huh... I'm freaking out. I think I'll go play basketball at church*?"

He laughed and squeezed her hand. "I said a prayer and your Dad showed up with a plate of muffins."

"What? I didn't know that."

"Yeah. He said he had a kid who was going stir-crazy being home for the break and asked if I wanted to go run it out at the church gym, too."

"Aww. Yay, Dad! That was cool. I never heard that part of it."

"And you were obviously an athletic girl and I should've been embarrassed, but you were nice about my lack of basketball skills. And fun to hang out with... and, I don't know. When I woke up the next morning, I was like, *I can do this. It's going to be okay*. And I started to feel like myself again."

"You *can* do this. It *is* going to be okay," she told him. "And I like who you are. I'm so glad you came, Boston. I hope I get to see you after..." She wasn't sure how to finish her sentence, so she shrugged and kept her eyes fixed on the road ahead of them. The Adam's house was coming up on the right.

Boston loosened his grip on her hand to lace his fingers with hers. "You will," he whispered.

Caught

BOS: are you asleep?

QUI: nope. why are you awake? Don't you leave early tomorrow?

BOS: yes

QUI: what's up?

BOS: we caught the ding dong ditchers

QUI: no way! who was it?

BOS: the little boy you brought over that once to play cards. Oliver

BOS: he and his mom

QUI: yay! you found them!

Her phone rang and she sat up, fixing the pillows behind her back before she answered. "Was Grandma surprised?"

"She acted like it, but I don't think she was. They stayed and talked for a while. Dad started asking questions and it turns out they don't have a lot of things in their apartment."

"It's true. They've gone through a lot in the last while."

"It sounds like it. Grandma offered a bunch of her furniture and all of the food storage and stuff that she can't bring to Nevada."

Tears pricked at Quincy's eyes. "That's amazing! Oh, I am so glad to hear that! It's really cool that Olly was your doorbell ditcher."

Boston was quiet for a few seconds. "It's funny. They have the same scarves that we do."

"Yeah?" Quincy felt caught. Was she caught?

"Mm-hmm."

"That's... great."

"And Grandma mentioned that you know how to crochet," Boston continued.

"Oh." Quincy cleared her throat. "Yes, I do."

"And Olly's mom? She told us how there was this girl at church who had been watching out for him while she was at work. And she crocheted the scarves."

Quincy was speechless. She thought they agreed that they would leave her name out of it and just let Olly get the thanks.

Boston continued, "And I just can't help but think that it would take an amazing person to come home for winter break and find someone to serve, first thing."

When Quincy didn't respond, Boston continued. "And you know, I saw this little boy, and his mom, so... *joyful* to have served my grandmother." Boston sniffed. "And knowing that this little ding dong ditcher was the reason my grandma was excited every day— it feels like a Christmas miracle. It gave her something to look forward to, and someone to love..."

Quincy sniffed and wiped a tear from her cheek.

"And I just can't help but think that I really want to keep that kind of girl in my life. It doesn't matter how long ago I met her."

A week. It had been a week. She had counted each day they had spent time together with a little heart on her calendar.

"Wow." Quincy cleared her throat and grinned. "That must be a really good scarf."

Boston laughed. "It is."

Natural

He said she'd recognize him as soon as she saw him, but she didn't see anyone who looked like how she remembered Boston looking in person. It had only been a month and a half. Besides, she saw him on video chats all the time. She should be able to recognize his dazzling smile anywhere.

Quincy turned the last corner and walked through the metal detectors and slipped by dozens of people waiting for deplaning passengers. She hitched her backpack higher on her shoulder and kept walking. He said he'd be waiting at her gate... there he was. The red scarf was the giveaway.

Boston was leaning against a thick round pillar, and his eyes followed Quincy until she cleared the waiting crowd. He pushed off the pillar and made a beeline for her, picking her up in a hug as soon as he was close enough to do so.

And then he kissed her.

"First kiss," he said, and laughed.

Then he kissed her again. "Second kiss," he murmured. "Mmm."

This time she laughed. "You're a natural," she teased.

"You bring out the best in me." He grinned and picked up her backpack and slung it over his shoulder. "C'mon, Quin. I promised Grandma I'd bring you by before I show you Vegas. Are you ready?"

She shook her head and refused to budge. "Nope. Third time's the charm."

Boston smiled widely and slowly leaned in to kiss her a third time. This time she kissed him back.

"Now I'm ready," she said, and took his hand. "Show me your world, Boston."

HOLIDAY GREETINGS

BY SHANNA L. K. MILLER

HOLIDAY GREETINGS

Ho, Ho, Ho and
here we go
Holiday greetings
all in a row.

Stacked on the
mantle, hung
on the wall
Friends and family
have come to call.

Plastered on
appliances, taped
to the door
Suspended by
string, Oops! one
fell to the floor.

We never know
what envelopes
may hold
But we're sure to
be pleased, truth
to be told.

Perhaps 5 X 7
glimpses of
color-coordinated
perfection?
(Which may or may not
be an accurate
reflection.)

There are verses with
rhyming, others just
signed.
Thanks for sending
them, you're
ever so kind.

Also appreciated
are your photos
with notes
Of comings and
goings and little
kids' quotes.

These capsules of
time reviewed again,
one by one
Are reluctantly
removed when the
season is done.

A quiet moment in
which we may pause
and reflect
In gratitude for
connections
that we should
never neglect.

Gathering our bounty,
we put them away
with a sigh
Keeping out some
favorites that
need a reply.

P.S. We're ever so
glad you kept us
on your list.
Please remember us
next year, we don't
want to be missed!

AN UNTRADITIONAL CHRISTMAS

BY CLARK GRAHAM

Harold Jones picked up the green tie and put it around his neck. It was Wednesday and he always wore the green tie on Wednesdays. He only owned five ties, one for each day of the work week.

He had taken over a rundown publishing business to become the largest publisher in town in just over ten years, doing it by being precise. Every press had a scheduled maintenance plan that had to be followed religiously. When a press was a certain age, it was replaced, no matter how well it was running. There were no breakdowns as a result. All presses were running a hundred percent of the time.

Harold scheduled all business three months in advance. He didn't like surprises. Even his breakfast was always the same. Two eggs, two slices of bacon and a piece of toast. The only thing he varied was the juice and milk.

He loved precision in everything he did, but today wasn't going well. It was Christmas Eve and he always took Christmas Eve off, except for this year. The city's annual Christmas Eve concert sold more tickets than they expected and they needed to double their order for programs.

Harold had thought about turning them down. He hated it when people couldn't plan ahead, but he knew his competitor would be more than happy to help them out. Grudgingly, he called in his workers and started up the presses.

Production was in full swing when he arrived. He didn't have to be there. His employees knew what they were doing, but they also knew if there was work to be done, Harold would be there.

They loved their boss. They all knew what they needed to do and what was expected of them.

They were treated well.

After the order was run, Harold delivered them and let the workers go home for Christmas. Even though he was all smiles when he arrived at the city offices, he was frustrated. He would be late.

He always went to his mother's house on Christmas Eve. To make matters worse, it was starting to snow, he didn't like driving in snow.

When he arrived home, his wife, Judy, met him at the door. "Honey, let's call your mother and tell her we can't make it. It's late and snowing. I can make a proper Christmas Eve dinner instead of all the candies and cookies she'll feed the kids."

He poked his index finger in the air, as he always did when he wanted to emphasize his point.

"Tradition is the key to the holidays. Without tradition, there is no holiday spirit."

The children, Bill and Ann, jumped up and down. They knew Grandma would spoil them with cookies and candies. Judy sighed and helped them put on their coats.

The thirty-mile drive was mostly on the interstate. Usually it only took forty minutes. This time, however, it took an hour. Harold was instantly happy he had made the trip, as his mother was delighted to see them. "I thought you weren't going to make it, with the snow and everything." She hugged each one of them in turn.

Games, popcorn, candy, and cookies occupied the evening. Two hours into the festivities, Judy looked outside. "Honey, the snow is getting deep. We should spend the night here. I don't want to drive in that."

Harold pointed his finger in the air again. "The children expect to spend their Christmas Eve in their own beds. Tradition is the key to the holidays."

She folded her arms. "We need to leave now then." Reluctantly, he agreed.

He had just turned the corner from his mother's house, when he saw the police car blocking the on-ramp. Harold rolled down his window as the officer walked up. "Terrible accident. The freeway's closed. It's best if you go back where you came from. You can go by way of the old highway, through Butcher's Holler, but I wouldn't recommend it."

It was the third time that Harold was given the advice to not drive that night and it would be the third time he ignored it. Butcher's Holler was just a collection of three old boarded-up buildings.

Since the freeway came through, no one passed by anymore. The butcher shop, general store, and restaurant all went out of business.

As Harold drove on, the wind picked up and the snow increased. It was piling higher and higher.

Years later Ann would claim the accident was because the dangerous curve sign was blocked by the snow. Bill would claim that his father was driving too fast for conditions. Either way, the car slid off the road and straight into a large oak tree. A crunching sound echoed through the valley as the windshield shattered, steam poured out of the hood, and the engine died.

After making sure that everyone was fine, Harold sat there contemplating what he should do. Judy tried to use her cell phone, but there was no reception.

"Hallo," came a voice from outside the car. "You folks okay?"

Ann looked out her window and exclaimed, "Santa Claus!" Before anyone could stop her she opened her door and ran out. Bill followed her, in a burst of excitement.

In fact, it wasn't Santa Claus at all. It was Jack Doyle. The portly old man with snow in his gray beard was surprised to be suddenly hugging two children. Judy ran out after the kids, but stopped when she encountered Jack.

"You folks okay? I came out when I heard the crash. Name's Jack."

Judy answered, "Yes, we're okay."

Harold was the last one out of the car. He looked the man up and down, trying to form an opinion. He wasn't good at making snap judgments though.

"Well, come on then. You'll freeze to death out here. I have a warm fire at least." Jack walked towards a dark house that seemed every bit as abandoned as the building they had just passed by.

Judy and Harold looked at each other, wondering what they should do. The children on the other hand, were already on their way, trailing closely behind Santa Claus. Having no real option, the parents followed along.

The house was old and unpainted. Harold wondered if he pulled a nail out would the whole thing crumble around him. But the wind had increased and the temperature was dropping so he went In. Candles were the only source of light, except for the fireplace. The family moved closer to it to take the chill out of their bones.

Harold heard Jack talking to someone on the phone. When Jack was finished, he came back in the room. "Sam's going to come pick up your car and will tow it into town, but not until the county plows the road. Looks like you're bunking here for the night. You folks hungry?" He didn't wait for an answer, but brought out two Dutch ovens and began cutting up food to put in them.

The children, after Jack brushed the snow out of his beard, realized he wasn't Santa, but he was still a nice old man, so they were okay with that. "Can I help?" Judy volunteered.

"Yep, you can peel the potatoes if you like." Jack handed her a knife and a sack of potatoes.

Harold was very upset. He paced back and forth. It was Christmas Eve and he had ruined every family tradition that they ever had by wrecking the car. He watched as a ham was put in the other Dutch oven and both of them were put into the fireplace.

"Power company decided to cut my electricity last month. Had a bad year with the crop failing and all. Couldn't pay my bills. I lost my Sherri in the fall. Married forty-five years when she passed. About to lose the house, too. Can't pay the taxes, neither." A tear rolled down Jack's cheek, but it was quickly wiped away. "It don't matter, I'm still good for one more Christmas. Haven't had visitors in a while. No one likes driving through Butcher's Holler anymore."

Dinner was ham, potatoes and greens. It was delicious in its simplicity. The kids, even though they were still half full of candy, had seconds. After the meal, Jack brought out blankets and pillows and they all curled up by the fire, while Jack read the Christmas story out of a tattered old family Bible.

Harold was lost in his own thoughts and feeling guilty about ruining the family's Christmas traditions as he settled under the covers on his makeshift bed near the fireplace. Sleeping fitfully, it wasn't until three in the morning that he noticed Jack wasn't there. He sat up and looked out the window. Footprints led away from the house to the garage. He could hear a generator going. Harold wondered what Jack was up to, but not enough to get out from under the covers. He turned over and settled back to sleep.

In the morning, Jack brought the kids each a handmade, brightly painted, soldier-shaped nutcracker. "Careful, paint might still be a little wet. Hasn't warmed up enough to dry yet." They both hugged Jack and he let out a deep-throated laugh.

An hour later, the snow plow came through and it wasn't long after when Sam and the tow truck arrived at the house. They all hugged Jack goodbye and went home to an abundant Christmas.

Two days later, Jack's power came back on. He also received notice that somehow his taxes were paid.

Every Christmas Eve from then on after visiting Grandma's house, was spent around the fire at Jack's in Butcher's Holler. The lights would be turned off and Jack would read the Christmas story by candlelight.

"After all," Harold would explain, finger pointing into the air, "Tradition is the key to the holidays."

A SMUGGLED CHRISTMAS: A VENUSIAN SKIES SHORT STORY

BY L. P. MASTERS

"I've got a question, Melli."

I glanced up from the pile of graphene and stifled a yawn as I looked at Ishaan. "Yeah?"

"Would this be considered stealing?"

I raised an eyebrow at Ishaan and then returned my gaze to the graphene rope. I lifted another length of it and inspected it to make sure it was the high quality we were looking for. "Why would you say it's stealing?"

"Well." Ishaan glanced at his watch. "We're working on this in the middle of the night, keeping it quiet from everyone else on the dirigible. And we're using the graphene fashioner without express permission. It kind of feels like stealing."

"Stealing what?" I asked, focusing harder than I really needed to on the graphene. "This rope is made out of carbon we're pulling out of the Venusian atmosphere. That's the whole purpose of this mission, to reduce the amount of carbon in the atmosphere. So I don't see why we shouldn't be using it for something useful."

"Hmm."

Ishaan inspected the line again for a few minutes in silence. I yawned again. This whole "doing things at night" stuff was getting to me. I was never a night owl. I was the kind of girl who needed my sleep. But I had no other choice. We couldn't let certain people know we were working on this project, and we had to get it done before the sun rose on Day 5.

"Got it," Ishaan suddenly said.

"What?"

"It's not stealing. It's smuggling."

I grinned at him.

He held up a finger. "We're smuggling Venusian carbon to create a secret rope."

"Exactly." I saw an imperfection; a little nick in the thin, gray line. "And we've got to make sure that secret rope is perfect." I pointed to the nick and Ishaan grabbed it, pulling it back over to the graphene fashioner to fill the gap.

I closed my eyes and leaned my head back against the wall. I guess now I was a Venusian Smuggler. Add that to my growing list of crimes.

***

The alarm went off right next to my ear. For a moment, I was back on Earth, with my annoying brother blowing an air horn in my face to wake me up. Then I realized I had fallen asleep with my face literally on top of my phone. I guess I figured it could act as a pillow. Good thing I didn't drool.

I turned the alarm off with my heart thundering beneath my ribs. I looked around, and found myself beneath a sort of blanket of graphene rope. When did I drift off? And why didn't Ishaan wake me up? My body ached from sleeping on the hard deck with nothing but a phone for a pillow.

I sat up, my bones cracking as I moved. I wasn't really that old, but after a night like that, I felt twenty years older than I was. Or twenty Venusian Days older, which was close to twenty years on Earth. This secret night time smuggling stuff was going to put me in an early grave.

I coiled up the rope again and covered it with the tarp. Ishaan always promised me that no one would find it here. He said he was really the only one on the NOVA dirigible who came into the graphene lab. Still, I didn't want it to be discovered.

I left the lab and stepped out into the hallway. To my right was the observation lounge and the storage room, a little hint of eucalyptus scent still tinting the air. To my left was the hall that would lead me to the stairs, but if I just kept going, I'd be right there in my garden, ready to start the day's work.

I could just skip breakfast. Again.

My stomach growled at me for having such a terrible thought and I frowned, walking to the stairs and heading up. My stomach was probably right. I really couldn't afford to be skipping meals, not with rationing still going on.

I got up one flight of stairs and was ready to step out into the hall when Randy came down from the flight above. My heart raced and I felt my eyes widen. Here I was in the wrong place... again... with Randy being witness to it.

He raised an eyebrow at me. "Good morning."

"Yeah," I said, then felt awkward. "Yeah" isn't really the proper response to "Good morning."

"Were you down on level one?"

"Mmm-hmm."

"Before breakfast?"

I shrugged. "I wanted to see how my seedlings were doing. Emory forgot to water them over my weekend and I came into work yesterday and they were parched. I was worried about them this morning. So I went down to check on them."

Guess what? I'm not a very good liar. I hated how much I'd had to do it lately.

One corner of Randy's lips came up. "You know something, Melli? You're kind of a workaholic."

I flashed a quick smile. "Yeah. I know." I stepped towards the door, ready to go to the cafeteria. Ready to sit down at the New Table with my friends and co-conspirators. Ready to talk more about how we were going to pull off this crazy idea—about how we were going to rescue an alien from the scorching, high pressure Veunsian surface. I was a workaholic. He didn't even know. But the addiction was to a work I wasn't getting paid for. It was to a work that most of the people on NOVA didn't even know I was engaged in. A work that people would probably call me crazy if they knew what it was.

Randy followed me out the door. He would probably follow me through the food line, too. But at least he wouldn't sit at the New Table. It was kind of a 'by invitation only' type of thing, and everybody in the cafeteria seemed to recognize that.

"So? How are they doing?" Randy asked.

My mind raced for a moment. How are my co-conspirators doing? How are the Venusian aliens doing? I glanced at him. "Who?"

"The seedlings."

"Oh!" I forced a smile. "They're fine. They'll pull through all right." The other problem with lying—you have to keep your story straight.

I kept walking towards the cafeteria, and he kept walking beside me. Maybe it was just my mind playing tricks, but I felt almost certain that he was inspecting me as closely as I had been inspecting the graphene rope.

My mind went wild, trying to tell me everything that was going on in his head. He was trying to see through my lies. He could tell I was lying, and he wanted to get to the bottom of it. And who could blame him? He was the head of Security on NOVA, and we still hadn't figured out who was sabotaging the dirigible. Some days I felt certain he didn't suspect me of sabotage. Some days I was in the wrong places at just the right times and I wondered how he could think it could be anyone other than me who was destroying crops, shutting off lights, popping holes in the walls, and creating chaos. I couldn't read human minds, and maybe that was a good thing. Randy wasn't the only one who suspected me of the sabotage, I was sure.

We stepped into the cafeteria and I took a deep breath, trying to clear my mind. I walked to Jonathon, who was overseeing rations that morning. He scanned my badge to ensure I hadn't already received my morning ration, and then he carefully watched to make sure I took only one serving.

Randy scanned his badge and grabbed his plate as well. I glanced at Jonathon and noticed he wasn't as intent on watching Randy as he'd been watching me.

Can't be trusted. That's what everyone on NOVA seemed to think of me. I'd given them plenty of opportunities not to trust me. I was always nearby wherever the sabotage was happening. And I always managed to say the wrong thing. I'd seen the looks on their faces, and I'd heard them whisper my name like conspiracy theorists trying to find proof. I'd been searching for the saboteur like everyone else was. But my reason for catching them was different. My reason for catching them was to prove I wasn't guilty.

I looked at the New Table, relieved to see it was already filling up with the people I knew. I was happy about the opportunity to get away from Randy's concerned eyes but just before I stepped away from him he touched me gently on the shoulder. "Melli, could you swing by my office after you finish work this evening? I need to talk to you about something."

I felt my cheeks flush, and wished they wouldn't. "Uh. Sure."

I quickly walked away from him and sat down next to Veronica.

The worst part about interacting with Randy was how unclear I was about what any of our interactions meant. Sometimes when I walked past the storage room and smelled the scent of eucalyptus that still drifted from there, I remembered what almost happened that day. I remembered Randy standing so close to me, thanking me for everything I'd done, saying he was sorry for everything I'd lost.

I remembered him almost kissing me. I remembered how conflicted I was about if I wanted him to or not.

And how I was almost disappointed when he didn't.

But ever since that day, there had been a much-needed distance between us. Shortly afterward there was an attempt on the Captain's life. Another instance of me in the wrong place at the right time. Another round of interrogations he put me through. And I felt guilty even though I knew I wasn't. Randy had actually thrown me in the NOVA's tiny jail cell for a day and a half.

I stabbed my fork into my meager omelet and took a bite. Veronica nudged me gently and said, "I see pink cheeks again. And I'm pretty sure I saw the tall, dark and handsome head of security standing next to you this morning."

"He asked to see me after work."

"Ooh! A repeat of the storage room, perhaps?"

"No. More likely him wanting to put cuffs on me and say he's finally found some proof that's connected me with all this insanity. And I can spend the rest of the mission in his jail cell."

Veronica rolled her eyes. "Oh come on. I'd give it a sixty-five percent chance that is *not* what he wants to talk to you about."

"Sixty-five?"

She shrugged, took a bite of eggs, then said, "What? Would you prefer it if I gave you sixty-seven percent?"

I scoffed at her, then said, "What have we found out from the atmospheric scientists? Do they think we'll even be able to drop the rope and basket?"

Veronica groaned. "You know what, Melli? You're kind of a workaholic."

I glared at her. "Yeah. I know."

But then she started talking about the atmospheric scientists, instead of the head of security, and that was fine by me.

***

Time for my afternoon power nap. I'd started taking those when I started staying up late. They didn't really seem to be helping that much. Especially since I didn't actually get any rest. Most of the time, my power naps were overpowered by Quanora connecting straight to my mind so we could work out more details of her smuggling the seeds into the rope and basket so we could grow her plants in the dirigible, instead of on the surface.

That day it wasn't any different. She wanted to know how the rope was coming. She wanted to know what the scientists had said. She started giving me more of the numbers that Rodge had asked for. Next thing I knew that darn alarm was squealing in my ear again. At least I hadn't used my phone for a pillow this time.

Fifteen minutes go fast when you're trying to save an entire alien species from extinction.

I put my air mask back on and stepped into the airlock to enter my garden. The plants there were so vibrantly green, which made sense as they were constantly flooded with CO_2. It was like Shangri-la for these beauties. But it was also heavy. When the saboteur had released helium from the buoy chamber beneath my garden, it had pulled the whole dirigible off balance. We didn't have enough helium to replace what we'd lost and I'd been forced to sacrifice two of my trees to rebalance the weight.

Ever since that day, I'd been careful to make sure I appreciated my garden more whenever I had the opportunity.

I knew there was work I needed to do; measurements I needed to take, notes on plant growth I should be writing. But all I wanted was to spend a little time with my true friends. The plants in my garden were like the children I never had. I wandered through the pathways that were crowded in by overgrowing leaves. I touched the leaf of a peace lily as I went past it, and admired the bright pink flower of a Christmas cactus that had just started blooming.

I made my way to the back section of the garden, where the roof was vaulted up into the second level of the dirigible and the trees grew as tall as two stories. My eucalyptus trunk was starting to put out new shoots, and I smiled. My oak tree wasn't doing very well, though, and that left a little pain in my chest. We'd pruned both trees to a dangerous extent and moved their wood into the storage room to redistribute the weight. I had been praying for the oak ever since the pollard pruning, and it seemed like my prayers weren't getting past the thick Venusian atmosphere.

I had to walk away from the two victims. I dried my eyes as a tear puddled at the top section of my mask. I moved on through the trees and saw that the tangerines were finally ripe, I knew in a few days Veronica would be in here to harvest them. I knew I shouldn't have, but I couldn't help myself. I reached up and plucked a tiny orange fruit off the branch and slipped it into the big pocket on the right leg of my pants.

Then I rounded the burning bush and saw the pine tree. Emory and Monty were both standing there, and I stopped, ducking back behind the burning bush.

They were talking to each other, but their voices were so low I couldn't hear what they were saying. And then I saw Monty hang something small and red on one of the branches of the pine tree. Emory laughed and pushed his shoulder gently. Then he said a little louder, "Couldn't let you miss another Christmas without the ornaments on the tree. The last two were hard enough on you."

I turned and walked back to the front of the garden. I walked back to where there was work to do; measurements to be taken, notes on plant growth to be written.

Christmas? Was it really Christmas?

On Venus we spent 90 hours in the daylight and 90 hours in the dark as our dirigible was pushed around the planet with the prevailing winds. On Venus we counted the Venusian Days of our mission by when the sun rose and set on a specific mountain on the surface of the planet. Venusian Day 5 was just around the corner, which meant that we were almost 3 earth-years into this mission.

But everyone always seemed to be talking about the next light or dark cycle, or what Venusian Day of the mission we were on. Everyone was talking about when their next weekend would be, or when they would get to take their next shower. I never heard people mentioning what day it was on Earth.

I knew someday we would go back there. But right now, it felt like we were completely disconnected from our home planet. And especially me. My workaholic tendencies, my stress about the sabotage, the Venusians, the rope, and my job. I didn't have time to think about Earth and what was going on there. And frankly, I didn't have much desire to think about it, either.

But it was Christmas? At least... Christmastime. How close to Christmas was it?

I shook my head and pulled out my phone to check Earth's calendar.

It wasn't just Christmastime. It was actually the day. Today was Christmas. Well, at least in one part of the world. It was Christmas Eve in America. But I still couldn't believe it. It snuck up on me like a smuggler.

***

I took a calming breath, then rapped gently on Randy's office door.

"Come in," he said.

I closed my eyes and hesitated a moment, then pushed through the door. "You asked to see me when I was done with work?"

"Ah. Yes. Thank you for coming by." His eyes drifted past me. "Shut the door. Why don't you come on in?"

I did so with dread, wondering if this was a trap. He wanted the door shut so it would be harder for me to run away when he told me he'd discovered something I'd done wrong. Maybe it was something I really had done wrong. Maybe it was him accusing me of the sabotage, which I hadn't done. Whatever it was, he wanted me trapped.

And then I felt my shoulders drop. Who was I kidding? I was already trapped. We were living on a dirigible with a total of three stories on it, surrounded outside by toxic air and acid rain.

Randy bit at his lower lip and glanced around uncomfortably. Here it was. He was about to drop the bomb. "Uh. Why don't you have a seat?"

I slumped into the chair like a criminal slumps into the witness stand.

Randy came around his desk and sat on the edge of it. "I... uh..."

My heart was thundering in my ears so loud I almost couldn't even hear him. And who would *want* to hear him. He was about to tell me that, even though he did have a crush on me once, he was going to have to put me in jail again.

And then he said, "It's Christmas. And I really shouldn't be..." His eyes danced around the room, resting everywhere but on me. "Well. I mean. I don't have a gift for everyone on the NOVA. Actually. I don't have a gift for anyone else on the NOVA... but you."

Finally, his eyes landed on mine, and that same intoxicating intensity I had felt from him in the storage room flooded back. That intensity that came right before the *almost* kiss. He reached into his pocket and left his hand there.

"I know that on occasion I have perhaps crossed boundaries that I shouldn't really have crossed. We're all supposed to be professionals here, and anything that makes our relationship seem anything more... intimate... well, we should probably avoid."

"We probably should," I agreed softly.

"Right. But..." He bit his bottom lip again and I smiled at what I had recently identified as a nervous habit. "But I made this specifically for you, and it doesn't seem right to not give it to you."

He pulled his hand out of his pocket, and with it came a little wooden figurine of a koala and its baby. The koala was about the size of a tennis ball. It fit almost perfectly in my palm.

"Wow," I said, taking the carving from him and looking at the intricate details cut into the wood.

"I was trying to figure out what to carve. I thought about a flower or a bird. But I can't think of eucalyptus without thinking of koalas."

My heart stuttered, and I brought the wood to my nose, drawing in a deep breath that was both sweet and spicy. "This... is my eucalyptus?" I asked.

He nodded, a big grin across his face. "Yeah."

I stared at the carving for another few seconds, then I looked up into his dark eyes and I narrowed my own eyes. "That wood was supposed to stay in the storage room to maintain balance in the dirigible."

The grin fell. "Oh. Yeah. It was."

"So, you smuggled it out of storage?"

He raised an eyebrow. "I guess so."

I grinned at him. "Aren't you supposed to be the head of security?"

Randy shrugged. "What can I say? I'm a terrible head of security."

I thought of everything we had gone through in the last several months, and I shook my head. "No. You're really not."

He frowned. "I haven't caught the saboteur yet."

"No. But you've kept us alive, despite their best efforts to do the opposite."

He looked at the ceiling. "I've had a bit of help."

I looked at the carving one more time and then decided I would put it in my pocket when I was ready to leave so no one else would see it when I went back to my room. But as I thought about my pocket, I felt a little lump pressing against my leg.

"Alright. I confess," I said.

Randy's eyes got big. He leaned slightly forward. He looked worried, as if he was the other part of sixty-seven percent certain I was about to tell him I was the saboteur.

I pulled the tangerine from my pocket and tossed it to him. "I'm a bit of a smuggler myself."

Randy laughed. Without hesitating, he dug a fingernail into the bright orange skin of the fruit and tore it open. "What's Christmas without a tangerine, right?"

"That's right." My mouth was watering as the citrusy scent filled the air.

He pulled off a section and put it in his mouth.

I got off my chair and stepped closer to him. "You're going to share that with me, aren't you?"

"What? You didn't bring two?"

I punched him on the shoulder and he chuckled, ripping the tangerine not quite in half and giving me the bigger piece.

I sat down beside him on the edge of his desk, holding the carving in one hand and admiring it, holding the tangerine in the other and savoring it. "Thanks for the carving."

"Thanks for the tangerine," Randy replied.

We sat in his office and ate the orange. I could smell the tangy sweet of the fruit, the spicy sweet of the wood, and the musky scents of Randy's aftershave all mingling together in a heady aroma.

Randy put his arm around my back, and both of us at the same time said, "Merry Christmas."

"Jinx," I said. Then popped another segment of tangerine in my mouth.

He was right. We needed to keep the relationship professional. But a carving and a shared tangerine on Christmas Eve between a couple of smugglers on Venus. Who could say no to that?

FIREHOUSE CHRISTMAS PARTY

BY DEB GRAHAM

"That's it, Ritchie. This time I've got you dead to rights. I'm calling the police. What kind of a man steals from kiddies at Christmas?" Ted Thompson, the neighborhood troublemaker and resident loudmouth, struggled under Ritchie's grasp.

"What are you doing, sneaking around in the dark like a common thug?" Dragging him from behind the bush into the light, Ritchie growled, "You want to know what I'm up to? Come and see. Heck, you can even help." He hauled the protesting man by the collar to his station wagon, stuffed with bulging sacks and boxes. Three other men ferried lumpy sacks onto a wheeled cart to the hospital entrance, not making eye contact with Ted.

"Lemme go! Johnny, is that you? Tom? You're in on this?" Ted yelled, "You won't get away with this, I can tell you that!"

"Gentlemen!" A nurse in a white uniform stepped out of the door. "Gentlemen, please! We have sick patients in here."

"Make yourself useful." Ritchie jammed a heavy box into Ted's arms. "Take this and mind you don't drop it. That's the cookies."

This story is about my father in the mid-1960s and it happened just this way, but first, you need to know about him.

Richard Abraham was a loud, outgoing, gregarious, hard-working man who loved his family and was fiercely loyal. He had a big, generous heart stuffed into his fire hydrant-shaped body. He also had a streak of mischief as wide as his head, often getting into scrapes no one else would. Born to immigrant parents, a first-generation American and the youngest of nine children, he grew up in serious poverty. The first time he owned two pairs of pants was when he joined the Army at age seventeen. His first job of work was at age eight, driving the horse-drawn milk wagon while Old Man Goldman delivered milk and dairy products to doorsteps, six hours a day before going to school. At age twelve, he took a job at a greengrocer. All the money he and his siblings earned, they gave to their mother, who ruled the household with an iron fist and sent the money her children earned to her brothers in the Old Country.

How would his childhood have been different had he been allowed to be a child instead of a worker at such a young age? It set the tone for the rest of his life, always working, expecting the same from others, but insisting "Kids need to be kids!"

When he had children of his own, Ritchie was the coach or umpire on their teams for many years. His career often required him to be out of town several days every week but everyone knew he'd never miss a game, even if he had to come straight from the airport to be there. The image of him parking with tires squealing, barreling across the parking lot, down the steep slope to the field, shouting "Let's take some practice, boys!" while throwing his necktie, suitcoat, and a quick kiss to Mom as he ran to get to his team on time is fresh in my mind. He shared homespun wisdom, including "Don't ever share your baseball glove or your underwear."

Each boy knew he could count on equal playing time on the field, regardless of skill level. Endlessly encouraging, he took time to bolster the weakest team members, making them feel like they really mattered, that the team needed them. By his example, the other players learned to cheer on their teammates, shouting, "You can do it!" and "You'll get 'em next time!"

The boys adored him. The fathers, less so. He would do anything to help and encourage those boys but had no tolerance for interfering parents. Red-faced dads berating their cowering sons for missing a ball or striking out during their turn at bat were promptly ejected from the games. Getting up in their faces, Ritchie made it clear "That's not how boys need to be treated, got it? We're raising men here." One year, he was an umpire and didn't hesitate to call out abusive coaches of teams when he didn't like the way they talked to their players, ejecting more than one.

He loved sharing stories and adventures, many of which were frankly not believable. As his daughter, I didn't believe most of his stories, including those I personally witnessed or was a part of.

In a random hotel elevator far from home one summer, a man fell all over him, pumping his hand, effusive in gratitude. For a minute, I was afraid he was going to kiss Dad. "You changed my life! If not for you, I'd have lost my family, my wife, my kids. I could have ended up in jail. Now I'm in a far better job, making great money, and I'm *happy*, all because of what you told me that day." He stepped out onto an upper floor and the elevator door closed.

"Who was that?" we asked. "What did you say to him?"

"I have no idea."

Ritchie was very social, happiest with people around him. He also loved to talk to people, whether in person or on the telephone.

In his 60's he had a gallbladder attack while he and Mom were traveling out of state and complications set in. After surgery, he was put into the intensive care unit of the hospital. Before long, the medical staff was concerned about his suddenly skyrocketing blood pressure and heart rate. Doctors couldn't figure out what circumstance had arisen in just half an hour. The doctors talked to his wife, expressing concern about his agitation, warning if it continued to soar, he could die.

She had a suggestion. "He doesn't like being alone; he likes being connected to people. Give him a phone."

"Phones are not allowed in the ICU," the doctors insisted.

"Then he's going to continue to be upset."

As an experiment, they ran a long phone line from the nurses' station. Within minutes, after Ritchie placed short calls to his siblings and children and a couple of friends, his vital signs stabilized. He was released the following day.

Ritchie was a people person, always willing to help a friend or a stranger. If he couldn't help, he likely knew someone who could. He was a larger-than-life character in a squatty body and his loud upbeat voice filled any room he entered. Many a friend said, "It's always a party when he walks in."

His favorite time of year was Christmas. As a child, his family didn't acknowledge Christmas or birthdays or any other holiday. He never had a toy of his own, or much free time to play with one if he had had one. The first year they were married, Mom gave him a metal toy truck. He loved it and enjoyed driving it around the kitchen floor. For years, even after they had children of their own, she gave him a toy for Christmas.

Out from under the thumb of his family of origin, Ritchie threw himself into celebrating Christmas with gusto and glee. He hung strands of bright lights and sought out the best tree, singing carols off-tune with jumbled lyrics and as loud as he could. "Deck the bows with balls and follies, fa la la la la la" was a favorite. He loved having people around and prepared for parties with obvious joy.

He loved his family above all else, but the Niagara Hose Company came in near the top of things that made him happy. Our blue-collar neighborhood in Western New York encompassed several square blocks where everybody knew everyone else and the fire station was the central hub. Our house, built by Ritchie, his father, and father-in-law after work and on weekends, shared a property line with the firehouse. Just about every father in the area was a member of the volunteer crew. When the siren sounded, every man on the street dropped what he was doing and ran to the station. If they made it there before the trucks pulled out, they clambered on, often yanking on boots and jackets and gear as the truck raced past. If they were late by even a second, they had to drive themselves, arriving at the fire call to be teased by their peers.

The men were a tight-knit group. They'd shovel one another's driveways during the heavy winter snows and, during the summer, we kids lined the curbs to watch them in the summer parades, playing "Never on A Sunday" with gusto and pride as they marched by, the brass buttons on their uniforms shining in the sunlight. It was the only song they knew.

One summer, the city added a chain-link fence around the fire station's parking lot, bordering our lawn on that side. Besides being the ideal place to be for the neighborhood kids after the plows cleared the winter snow from the parking lot and piled it against the fence, making high mountains designed for tunneling, the aforementioned fence line was an issue for Dad more than once.

Ritchie worked rotating shifts at the factory; two weeks on day shift, two weeks on night shift, and he often took naps to ease the transition. Mom said he had run into the firehouse fence during the night soon after it was installed, but no one saw him. That next summery afternoon, he had far more witnesses than he wanted. About fifteen kids were playing ball in our front yard that afternoon, watched over by a handful of mothers chatting on the wide front porch.

The fire siren sounded, blaring through the neighborhood. Ritchie woke from a very sound sleep and barreled down the staircase, ran out the front door, across the front lawn, and hit the new chain link fence like it wasn't there. The fence held firm, bouncing him back a good ten feet, as if he'd struck a trampoline surface. He lay there stunned in the grass, staring at the blue sky, dazed and still not a hundred percent awake, as the firetruck raced by, his buddies jeering. Yes, I'm afraid his audience applauded as he dragged his sore body to the car.

Nobody missed a fire call.

Another time, he was again asleep in the middle of the day, probably having worked the night shift. We kids were watching *Batman* with our friends in the living room at the bottom of the stairs. The fire claxon sounded and he leaped up, bolting across the bedroom floor before he was fully awake. He yanked his shirt over his head and grabbed his trousers on the run. Tangled in his sleeves and blinded by the fabric, he tripped at the top of the stairs, did two complete somersaults down the steps, raced across the living room in his socks, out the door, across the lawn, and scaled the fence, making a flying leap onto the firetruck seconds before it reached the street. I can still see that image in my mind of him hanging on with one hand, wearing undershorts and half of a shirt, his trousers flapping in his other hand.

The firehouse, besides being a working fire station, was the social center of the area. At least for men; women and children were only allowed inside on the first Saturday of each month, New Year's Eve, and at the annual Christmas party. Although the wives complained mightily, that policy held well into the early 1970s. A monthly fundraiser was Fireman's Chowder, sold on the first Saturday of each month, minus the bitterly cold winter months. I never heard the numbers, but it had to have brought in several thousand dollars each month, perhaps more.

The volunteers at the firehouse (pretty much every man in the neighborhood) began preparing the rich soup in the firehouse parking lot on Thursday after work. Years before, someone had constructed one-hundred-gallon cast iron vats with wood fire chambers underneath to cook the chowder. As they cut up and added more ingredients at prescribed intervals, the soup expanded from one vat to two and then to three and four. Fifty-pound sacks of onions, carrots, potatoes, whole chickens, slabs of beef, giant cans of beans and tomatoes, water from the firehoses, and a few other things combined into a thick delicious chowder. It required constant monitoring through the night and all the next day, necessitating several shifts of men to be on-site in the parking lot to stir the soup, feed the fire, and chop more ingredients to add at the right time. This task was accomplished with plenty of beer and the use of poker chips.

By nine o'clock Saturday morning, the soup was pronounced Done and people lined up around the block, holding empty pots and bowls. The soup was sold by the bowl for twenty-five cents and three dollars for a gallon. It sold out every week before eleven o'clock and most families could count on that for their Saturday supper. Some people lingered, buying bowls of steaming chowder to eat on site, one of the very few times women and children were allowed into the fire station. Even as a child, I didn't see the big deal. The place was dim, vaguely greasy, and smelled of stale beer.

The chowder was delicious. I had my father write down the recipe when I was an adult. On a smaller scale, it required only a couple of hours cooking time, but still expanded to three Dutch ovens and filled my freezer. The recipe he gave me is at the end of this story. In varying forms, Fireman's Chowder is prepared and sold at some western New York fire stations to this day. Recipes are still hotly contested: to add winter squash or not? Is pork allowed or only beef? What about cabbage? Lima beans?

The chowder was important for another reason, beyond feeding the community it brought together. The cash raised from the soup sales was earmarked for two purposes: Charity and the Christmas party. "Charity" was a topic heatedly discussed over poker games at the station on Friday nights. What needs were deemed pressing enough to reach into the coffers?

When the Lewis' ice house caught on fire and its sawdust-filled walls smoldered for a week, the Lewis family was displaced. The fire department put them up in a motel until it was safe to go home. Not a good one, mind you, but adequate. Charity was not to be spent frivolously.

Mr Olivetti, down the block, had contracted malaria when he was working on the Panama Canal. He had periods where he was well enough to work and other times he was as sick as when he first contracted it, bed-ridden and sweating, out of his mind with fever. His wife was one of the few employed mothers I knew, a part-time nurse who could only work sporadically, due to taking care of her husband and young family. When he was ill, the fire station Charity Fund stepped in, paying their rent and electric bill, having a load of coal delivered for the furnace, and quietly slipping tearful Mrs Olivetti an envelope of dollar bills to buy food for the children.

Another Charity case was hotly debated. Mr Kurtzworth across the street was a belligerent alcoholic, a mean drunk who couldn't hold a job and beat his wife and children when he "tied one on." Although the men in the neighborhood did all they could do to intervene, from counseling with him to visiting him when he was sober and beating him up "so he knows what it feels like," the man was an unrepentant drunkard, no two ways around it. The Kurtzworth family had eight children under the age of teens and the subject of Charity was discussed repeatedly over rounds of poker. The man was a bad influence and a danger to his family. Yet his children needed to eat and the mother couldn't take a job of work, not with the kids so young and her in the family way again.

The firefighters eventually agreed to help the family with the Charity Fund long-term, on the condition the man of the house move into the garage for a while to cool off and realize what he'd be missing out on if he didn't straighten up. The decision came in February during a bitterly cold winter in the snow belt. Surprisingly, once she felt some support from the men of the neighborhood, his wife stood with the firefighters as he moved out, first to the garage, then to his mother's house, then he disappeared, as far as anyone knew. That family thrived and Mrs Kurtzworth was always near the front of the chowder line on Saturdays with a couple of soup pots and a few dollars, eager to pay it back as best she could.

At the end of the year, whatever Fireman's Chowder money was left after Charity expenses and chowder ingredient purchases was earmarked for the annual children's Christmas party. The highlight of every year, the party was headed up by whoever was the designated volunteer fire chief for that year. The fire chief post changed every two years, rotating through the men by popular vote. Every firefighter was expected to help out in large or small ways, on assignment from the chief.

As a child, I recall hearing the grownups saying one man had refused the honor because he had taken a demanding new job right before his wife delivered the premature twins. The men never looked at him quite the same after that, murmuring about him over backyard poker games. Where did his priorities lay?

The year I turned seven, Ritchie's turn as volunteer fire chief rolled around. Besides the obvious tasks of taking the lead at fighting fires, dealing with administrative things like training and money management, overseeing the chowder events, ordering enough snacks for the poker games, he was also in charge of the annual Christmas party.

Every child in the several-block area looked forward to the Christmas party. But with Ritchie Abraham in charge, this year would be even better. They all knew he loved Christmas, loved it more than anyone else around. They watched him festoon our house with lights, hauling home a huge Christmas tree the day after Thanksgiving, singing loudly and off-key starting in early November. He loved children and he loved Christmas and now was his chance.

Who better to head up the party? This year's party was going to be epic, everyone just knew it.

As was standard protocol, Ritchie enlisted the mothers in the neighborhood to bake mountains of cookies for the party, quietly dropping off sacks of flour and sugar and pounds of butter after dusk to those whose grocery budgets he suspected might be overtaxed by the request. He bought cases of candy canes and crates of oranges.

Wanting to be sure each neighborhood child received a gift from Santa, as they did every year, he solicited donations from local businesses, reminding them who their customers were and talking about goodwill in return for generosity. Did he suggest firefighters might be slower to respond to places that didn't donate, should a need arise? Who could say for sure?

In years past, while the elementary school music teacher played Christmas carols on the rickety piano in the corner and somebody's mother led a sing-along, a cotton-bearded Santa Claus in a somewhat beer-scented red velvet suit called each child up by name to sit on his lap. Magic; how did he know their *names*? Each child recited their memorized wish list before they chose a wrapped gift marked either Boy or Girl. The gifts were small trinkets: a yoyo, a ball, a plastic necklace, metal cars, a Slinky, a compass, maybe even a set of jacks, purchased with the Chowder Fund proceeds.

Ritchie's gregarious nature and fun-loving attitude drew people in like fish in a net. Most of the people he knew loved him and would do anything for him. No one believed most of his stories, even the ones they had personally witnessed; he had a way of attracting adventures and mishaps in equal measure. Regardless of the outcome, almost everyone wanted to be part of whatever scheme he had cooked up this time. As the year progressed and the plans unfolded, grander with every telling, his fellow firefighters were onboard with whatever he had planned for the Christmas party.

Except for Ted Thompson.

Ted took a dim view of the world in general and an even dimmer view of Ritchie in particular. Ted was usually the lone dissenting voice in the Charity Fund discussions, vetoing every suggestion, insisting no one had helped *him* so why should anybody help anybody else? If families were struggling, they deserved what they got. And if there had to be a Christmas celebration at all—he was opposed to that, too—he said children could stop by at a designated hour and pick up a candy cane at the door, *one each*, and be on their way, so long as they were quiet about it. No call to spend good money on treats or clutter the firehouse with glitzy decorations and all that folderol.

As for music, was there no way to shut Ritchie up? All that singing got on his last remaining nerve. A man that happy wasn't to be trusted.

Ritchie went ahead with his plans, either unaware of Ted's opinion or, more likely, choosing to ignore it. We kids watched the comings and goings in the days preceding the party with increasing excitement. What was inside all those boxes and lumpy bags? Had there ever been a Christmas tree that big? Those baskets surely held some magic. After all, Mr Abraham was in charge this year and every kid knew it. So much secrecy surely promised something incredible, for he excelled in the unbelievable. What kind of magic would he conjure up? Real reindeer, perhaps a few of Santa's elves? Sworn to secrecy, the dads who helped with the project were mum.

On the afternoon of the party, mothers carried cardboard trays of frosted Christmas cookies to the rear door of the firehouse. At last, after an early supper everyone was too excited to eat, the time had come. Dressed in their Sunday best—rumors said a real photographer had been hired!—families made their way to the firehouse. More snow was falling, and in the frigid air, the warm greetings exchanged by friends and neighbors added to the glittery night.

Parents nervously recalled that year—was it five or six years ago?—when a fire call came in right in the middle of serving the eggnog. The men ran to the truck and the women kept the party going as best they could, with singing and cookies, but every child had seen Santa leap on the fire truck with all the dads. The youngest ones cried, sure they'd miss out on a gift that year. Not to fear; Santa hurried back in Johnson's borrowed station wagon before the party dispersed. Reeking of smoke, he gave each child a toy and listened to them dictate what they'd like for Christmas. The party was memorable, but it was saved. Surely nothing like that would mar this year's party, not with all the effort and planning the crew under Ritchie Abraham's watch had put into it!

The door swung open and the children tromped down the stairs into the gallery, one level down from where the fire trucks were parked. The first children entered a fairyland, freezing in their tracks at the door, pushed forward by impatient people behind them. More Christmas lights than they'd ever seen in one place, strung from end to end of the ceiling, gave the dank hall a magical glow. Not one, but *three* Christmas trees stood sentry, their branches decorated with aluminum tinsel and glossy red ornaments. Tables laden with craft supplies beckoned the children. Construction paper, glue, even glitter! Glitter was a forbidden item in most homes, as mothers insisted it'd never come out of the carpet.

Music blared from a record player in the corner, every Christmas record Mr Abraham could find. He had assigned Mr Olivetti, the malaria patient, to change the vinyl records. Olivetti beamed, grateful to have something important to do to help out, without taxing his meager strength. Games beckoned children from every corner. As forecast, a photographer waved children over for a picture beside one of the trees. Against the back wall, a red velvet chair with gold trim stood waiting for Santa's arrival, and around it were heaps of big wrapped presents, promising far larger loot than the expected trinkets. Once the initial shock wore off, children raced in, laughing, dancing with excitement, kicking off snow boots and coats.

The party was on!

The first hour passed in a spirit of delight, with crafts and music and a sing-along, even a jazzy Christmas dance performance led by young Miss Lancaster, the pretty new dance teacher the women warned their husbands about. She could be a floozy; you never know. A long table groaned under heaps of decorated cookies and a massive punch bowl. For once, no parent scolded a child for eating too much sweet stuff, not at the Christmas party.

Suddenly, a bell tinkled. The time had come! The children scrambled to sit on the rug. Silence fell as Santa Claus, complete with a gorgeous red velvet suit and flowing beard that might have been real—who was brazen enough to yank on it?—came down the stairs. He took the microphone and bellowed, "Ho, ho ho!"

Sitting cross-legged on the fire station floor with their fruit punch and cookies, the sixty or so children stared, wide-eyed. The youngest ones shrank back. After all, they hadn't seen Santa in a full year, and hadn't Mother warned them about strangers?

"Ho, ho, ho! Merry Christmas! Here's the way it's gonna be. You listening? I know you kiddies all been waiting to talk to Santa and that's fine. But I have me a headache from too much...er, eggnog. I'm in no mood to hear you 'uns telling me I want, I want, I want. Not today."

The parents lining the walls eyed one another uneasily. What was Santa up to? This was not The Way Things Were Done. Who was he, anyway, in that fancy suit? Not from the neighborhood, that's for sure.

Whoever he was, he'd better not ruin Christmas!

Santa hitched up his red trousers. He was a beanpole of a man, not as jolly-shaped as the one in the children's books, and even with pillows under his red suit, things kept threatening to fall down. He made eye contact with every child then heaved a big sigh into the microphone.

"Listen up, you hear me? I'm a busy man and we're not wasting time today. I know every last one of you is going to write out your wish lists, maybe even add some pictures cut from the Sears Roebuck catalog, and send them up the chimney at your house. Those of you with no fireplace, you can feed it to your coal furnace; it'll reach the North Pole just the same and my elves will make sure I see your wish list. Not today. I'm not of a mind to hear about what anybody wants today."

Tears filled a few eyes. Someone sniffed. Several wiped their noses on nearby sleeves. The children had been so eager, rehearsing for days what to tell Santa what they wanted for Christmas. And now...

"We're doing things different," Santa went on. "What Santa really needs is some *help*. The elves are so tied up making toys, I can't count on them. I need some help brightening the world and making things easier for others. Spreading Christmas cheer, you know what I mean? You're a fine-looking bunch of kiddies and you're all big enough to help." He *ho ho ho'd* some more then hollered, "Where are my helpers?"

Every little upturned face stared at Santa with round eyes while their parents held their collective breath.

After a very long minute, a ten-year-old boy stood up and said, real loud, "Santa, I could be your helper. If I did my chores without complaining, that'd be a help, right?"

Santa bellowed a "Ho, ho, ho!" and waved the boy forward. "Terrific! That's exactly the kind of help I need. Merry Christmas! Come get a candy cane."

The other children caught on right quick. Soon there was a line of young ones, all eager to tell Santa what they could do to be his helper. Mind the baby, help Mother with supper, make up their bed, bring in extra coal for the furnace, help carry in the groceries, use their manners, on and on. With each child, the smiles grew bigger, the children more excited. Santa encouraged them to come up with new and different ways they could be of some use, and gave them each a high-five and a big candy cane. Every last one of them walked back to their seat on the rug grinning and feeling good about their offer to help.

And not one parent complained.

"Now we got that business out of the way, let's see if I have any presents for you today." Santa headed for the red velvet chair with the gilt arms. "We're going to keep the Christmas spirit going, right?"

The children squirmed in their places on the floor, eager but polite, awed by the heap of gifts by the Christmas trees. In years past, Santa had handed out trinkets like slinkies and yoyos, hair bows and jacks sets, but the pile of wrapped presents under the tree was so big this year, the boxes didn't fit under the tree; most of the colorful gifts were stacked against the wall. And those boxes were much too large for a superball, the hot new toy of the year. What could they be?

As names were called and wrapping paper shredded with glee, parents met one another's eyes with questions. What had Abraham done to get this kind of presents donated? Beautiful dolls with ruffled dresses, the newest board games, metal cars and race car sets, fancy paint sets with a folding easel, baseball mitts made of real leather. Gifts this size only appeared on Christmas morning.

Cries of delight filled the hall as one child after another shouted, "It's just what I wanted!"

Parents murmured, "Ritchie really outdid himself this time!" They figured he must have solicited donations from the local department store; the Chowder Fund couldn't have stretched half that far.

At last, every child had opened a gift. They polished off their cups of fruit punch (red; another forbidden treat at home because do you know what red punch does when it's spilled? It's a stand-in for those packets of Rit dye; everyone knows that) and mothers bundled their youngsters into snowsuits and mittens. Each beaming child recited, "Thank you for the nice party" on their way out of the fire station, clutching their new doll or truck or game.

The dads began wadding wrapping paper into trash bins, and Mr Olivetti turned off the phonograph. The men worked to restore the firehouse to its usual condition, sans lights, glitter, and cookie crumbs. Everyone agreed the party had been a fine success, better than any previous one.

Someone asked, "Ritchie, what do you want to do with the leftover presents?"

"Huh. We got leftovers? How many we got? I made sure to get a few extra in case somebody brought their cousin or a kid from school. I didn't want any sad girls and boys. Let me think." A moment later, he snapped his fingers. "Okay, everybody, load up my car. Take the leftover cookies and punch, too. Grab those paper cups. Johnny, can you stuff that smaller Christmas tree in your station wagon? Whatever presents don't fit in my car, put in George's or Gary's. I'll make a phone call. Move it, men."

Used to working fires together, they formed a bucket brigade, passing bags of presents and trays of cookies man to man, up the stairs and into the cars, rapidly filling four station wagons to the brim.

No one noticed Ted Thompson standing to one side, glowering. Ted didn't like Ritchie and he didn't trust him, not as far as he could throw a grand piano over the wide Niagara River. For all he knew, Ritchie was liable to sell those toys and keep the money. He was up to something, and Ted was going to ferret it out. He'd take down Abraham, once and for all.

Tonight was the night.

Within minutes, the firehouse was ship-shape, as ship-shape as tired men could manage on a timeline, what with Ritchie goading them on. "Come on, men! Taking down the lights can wait. We have to get there before bedtime and it's already dark."

Get where before whose bedtime? No one knew and no one asked. Ritchie clearly had a plan in mind.

"That'll do for now." Ritchie scanned the firehouse. "We can mop the floor later. Move out, men."

The men hustled up the stairs and into the cars. Ritchie led the way down Franklin Street and across the Niagara River Bridge, up the hill to the sprawling hospital complex overlooking the town. They parked the cars in a row and the men stamped their feet in the frigid air while Ritchie hurried inside to talk to the staff.

Another car pulled in around the corner, its lone occupant keeping to the shadows.

A couple of minutes later, two doctors in white scrubs followed by four nurses with jaunty caps pushed wheeled carts into the parking lot, led by Ritchie. All wore broad smiles. The firefighters loaded the carts with presents and decorations. Someone had even remembered to bring the record player from the station. Mr Olivetti clutched several Christmas albums under his arm. They quietly trooped into the hospital, ferrying the loot in the freight elevator and down the hall to the wide double doors marked Children's Ward on the third floor.

As Ritchie made his second trip to the parking lot, Ted Thompson stepped from the shadows, his fists raised. "That's it, Ritchie. This time I've got you dead to rights. I'm calling the police. What kind of a man steals from kiddies at Christmas? You're going to sell those toys, make a buck, aren't you? Not on my watch!" Ted Thompson, the neighborhood troublemaker and resident loudmouth, struggled under Ritchie's grasp. "Lemme go!"

"You big galoot! What are you doing, sneaking around in the dark like a common thug?" Dragging him from behind the bush into the glow from a streetlight, Ritchie growled, "You want to know what I'm up to? Come and see. Heck, you can even help, since you're here." He hauled the protesting man by the collar to his station wagon, stuffed with bulging sacks and boxes. Three other men reloaded the carts with wrapped boxes and lumpy sacks, avoiding eye contact with Ted.

"Johnny, is that you? Gary? You're in on this?" Ted yelled, "You won't get away with this, I can tell you that!"

"Gentlemen!" A nurse in a white uniform stepped out of the door. "Gentlemen, *quiet*, please! We have sick patients in here."

"Make yourself useful." Ritchie jammed something into Ted's arms. "Take this and mind you don't drop it. That's the cookies."

Ted paused only a minute before following the men into the brightly lit hospital, tin foil covering the frosted cookies Ritche had handed him. Confused, he stamped snow from his shoes and trailed Johnny and Gary up the stairs where a pile of gifts and treats and decorations had been amassed in the corridor. The firefighters shuffled their feet, unsure of what to do next.

A minute later, Santa Claus skidded down the hall, hitching up his red velvet trousers. "You didn't start without me? Good! I hit every red light on the way over and I didn't think using my lights and sirens was appropriate."

"Commissioner, is that you in that get-up?" The men straightened. "Back at the station, we couldn't tell for sure."

"Santa Claus, at your service. When your chief here called me, I was delighted to step in for the party at the station. This, men, is the icing on the cake. Or the Christmas cookies, in this case." He stroked his long white beard. "Chief Abraham, are you ready to move out? Yes? Fall in, men!"

At a nod, two nurses swung the double doors wide and Santa led a procession into the children's ward. The young patients gasped, unable to believe their eyes. Their backs ramrod straight, the firefighters hauled in the wrapped gifts, piling them in the middle of the floor where Johnny hastily set up the Christmas tree he'd crammed in his car, the tinsel barely crushed.

Ritchie shouted, "Merry Christmas, everybody! Who's ready for a Christmas party?" with a huge grin.

Nurses circled the room with trays of cookies, passing them out to the young patients, wide-eyed in their beds. One of the doctors poured punch into paper cups and the other distributed them from a tray designed to hold medicine.

"One of you nurses," Ritchie called out, "how about you get a sing-along started while Santa visits with the kiddies?"

A young nurse nodded at Mr Olivetti, who cranked up the phonograph. Soon "Rudolph The Red-Nosed Reindeer" rang through the ward. Some of the children were too weak to sing but every one of them wore a broad smile. All the old familiar carols filled the room, one after the other. Somehow, the beeping of the machines added to the music.

Dads themselves, the firefighters spread out, sitting by the children's beds, steadying a cup of punch, patting a hand, offering Christmas cheer with suddenly gruff voices. Their own children would sleep safe in their beds at home tonight, unencumbered by wires and tubes and plaster casts.

Santa made his way to each child, stroking the children's heads and whispering encouragement, listening to their wish lists with great patience, as if he had all the time in the world. When he finished at the bed of a little boy with his leg in traction, he exclaimed, "These are good children, very good indeed! Let's see what Santa has for each of them, shall we?"

The firefighters scrambled to their feet and gathered by the Christmas tree, awaiting orders. Santa directed the men to pick a gift, take it to each child, and help them unwrap it if they were unable to do it themselves.

Cries of delight rang out as the children realized the gifts were for them, not mere decorations like the shiny ornaments on the walls.

"My favorite!"

"I love it!"

"Oh, it's just what I wanted!"

"It's perfect!"

"For me? Wow!"

From a corner where he'd taken up a post after entering the ward-room, Ted Thompson folded his arms and muttered to Ritchie, "These aren't the same gifts the kiddies at the firehouse got. What did you do different?"

"What do you mean?"

"They're not the same. These are all quiet toys, the kind a boy or girl could play with in bed if they had to, not the kind they'd run around with." He ticked them off on his fingers. "A doll, a board game, a Slinky, a puzzle, not footballs and badminton rackets. That girl over there has one of those new Etch-A-Sketches. She can use it lying down. Good thing, since both of her legs are in casts. How did you plan that?"

"Look at these children. Really look at them." Ritchie kept his voice low. "If they could run around like regular kids, they wouldn't be here at the hospital. They're having a tough time of it. Giving them a soccer ball or hula hoop would make them feel worse. That girl with all the bandages, the nurse told me she pulled a pan of hot cooking oil from the stove down on herself. The little tyke over there, his dad ran a red light and hit a truck. What is he supposed to do with a new baseball mitt when he's all busted up?"

"Yeah, but the presents! How'd you do that?" Ted eyed Ritchie. "How did you know how many kids were in the children's ward tonight? How did you know which toys would be left over?"

"It's the Christmas spirit, man. I keep telling you you need to have a little faith, get with the program. Here, go see if anybody wants another Christmas cookie."

Ted shook his head. "This isn't my kind of thing."

"It is now." Ritchie shoved him.

"I know you're up to no good." Ted dug his heels in. "I just can't figure it out yet."

Santa, scanning the room, hurried over and took Ted by the arm. "I hear you're not a Christmas spirit kind of fellow. Is that so?"

Ted sputtered, "Commissioner, Abraham here is up to something. I just know it. He–"

"Yes, he is." Santa held up his hand to forestall another comment. "He's up to a real Christmas miracle and it'd do you good to get onboard. Now. *Capisce?*"

Ted nodded and slunk to the bed of a little girl, maybe four years old, with a thick white dressing on her head. She reached out her hand and asked softly, "Mister, can you help me open this present? I can't bend my hand. The cast is in my way."

He nodded and pulled the paper free. "Here you go. It's a stuffed dog."

"For me?" She clutched the plush animal as sudden tears filled her eyes. "It looks *just* like Sandy. Sandy is my dog. He got dead in the car crash. So did my big brother Joey." She sobbed into the stuffed animal's fur. "And now they are gone. Mommy told me."

A nurse hurried to the child. With a bright smile, she said, "What a sweet little doggy. Lucy, it's time for sleep now. Your new friend will stay here with you and rub your back until you nod off, all right?"

Ted blinked. What did he know about soothing a grieving child to sleep? He awkwardly patted her heaving shoulder, his eyes seeking escape anywhere in the room. Slowly, her hiccupping sobs subsided. Across the ward, Ritchie looked up from a Tiddlywinks game he was playing on a boy's bed. Their eyes met. Ritchie nodded.

"Mister, will you sing to me?" Lucy's eyes were already closed, tears drying on her cheeks, both arms wrapped around the stuffed dog.

He cleared his throat. If the guys heard him singing to a child, they'd razz him for weeks. In a low voice, Ted sang the words to a song he'd learned at his mother's knee when he was no older than Lucy. "*Silent night, holy night, all is calm...*"

As he rubbed the little girl's back, Ted surveyed the room. His buddies, gruff blue-collar workers all, moved from bed to bed, smoothing a blanket here, stroking a cheek there. One of the nurses dimmed the overhead lights, and in the glow of the Christmas tree in the center of the sterile room, the men he'd known for years looked like angels to him. He blinked to clear the image. A warm feeling came over him, something he hadn't felt since he was a child, as young as some of these broken children.

Was it the Spirit of Christmas? Was this what all the fuss was about?

Soon Lucy drifted off, the stuffed doggy tight in her arms. Ted continued to sit beside her bed, marveling at the feeling of peace in the large room. Time passed—he didn't know how much, caught up in the sweet spirit of the hospital children's ward. He startled at the touch of a hand on his shoulder.

"You coming? These kiddies need to sleep and the nurses want us out. The other fellows are already downstairs." Ritchie handed Ted the phonograph, closed in its case, its music stilled. "Take this."

"Yeah, I'm coming." Ted stood, carefully, so as not to disturb young Lucy.

On the way down the stairs, Ted ventured, "I still don't understand. How did you get the right toy to the right child? I didn't see any tags on them. The men just grabbed a gift, yet every gift suited that child perfectly. Little Lucy just lost her brother and her dog, and that stuffed doggy was exactly what she needed. And that boy with the airplane book—I heard a nurse saying he is crazy about airplanes."

"It's not all me, that's for sure." Ritchie shrugged. "I didn't even plan on being here tonight. When we had so many leftover presents, I figured the hospital could use them, give the kiddies some Christmas cheer. While the men cleared the station, I called the head nurse and she said to come on over."

"You didn't plan this? How did you have exactly the right number of presents for the children? They each got one but there are none left over. And the punch and cookies. How was there enough for the party at the station and the children's ward?"

"It just worked out that way."

"Abraham, that's why you do all this, isn't it?"

"For the miracle? Absolutely. I wouldn't miss it."

"Do you think—is there any way—" Ted stammered.

"Speak up, man."

"Can I help head up the Christmas party next year?"

The end of the story? Gruff old Ted Thompson was a changed man, changed by the Christmas miracle he experienced that cold wintery night. Every year afterward, at every firehouse Christmas party, that story of the night when the extra gifts were delivered to a second, impromptu party at the hospital was retold, and for once, no one needed to embellish the telling.

Ted jumped in to help with the following years' parties, contributing ideas no one else came up with. He also had a knack for bushwhacking local businesses for donations, insisting, "It's for the kiddies. Don't be such a cheapskate or you'll miss out on the Christmas Spirit."

And when Ritchie Abraham came up with his next harebrained scheme, and the many that followed, Ted was always first to volunteer to help. He became Ritchie's most devoted sidekick.

Do I believe in Christmas miracles? I absolutely do, for I saw a man transformed by one when I was a little girl, not much older than Lucy.

Niagara Hose Firehouse Chowder

Circa 1960s

This recipe is in my father's words as he told me. The chowder will fill two, maybe three, large Dutch ovens or stockpots before you're done. It takes an afternoon to simmer everything, not the two or three days the firehouse used. The tomatoes are 28-ounce cans; the other vegetables are 14.5-ounce cans, not drained. He meant a whole stalk of celery, not just one rib. The thick soup freezes well.

In one large pot, boil one **whole chicken** in enough **water** to cover it and put a lid on it the whole time. In another big pot, boil a three- or four-pound **chuck roast** and two or three pounds of **oxtail**. Cook until the meat falls off the bones. Strain the broth to get the bones out and let the meat cool on a platter. If you want, you can throw in some ice cubes to make the fat easy to skim off. Add in four cans of **whole tomatoes**, broken up, along with the juice in the can. Ten cups of cut up **onions** go next, with five pounds of diced **potatoes**, peeled first, and a whole bunch of **celery**, sliced. Cut the meat into bite-sized pieces and return to the pots. Simmer another couple of hours. Add in three cans each of **corn, peas**, and **green beans**, with their juice in the can, and add in two cups of **water**, too. Stir, making sure each pot has about the same ingredients, so one doesn't have all chicken and the other all the beef. Expand to another pot if it's too full to stir. Cook another hour or so, then season with enough salt and pepper.

Serve with **oyster crackers** but not too many. You don't want to soak up all the broth.

Grandma's Glorious Gifts

By Shanna L. K. Miller

Once upon a childhood Christmas, there was a grandmother, beloved by her family. Affectionately dubbed *GaGa* by her oldest grandchildren, she was simply called *Grandma* by the rest of us. A vivacious and diminutive dynamo, she stood just under five feet tall in her stocking feet.

Grandma was a trailblazer. What she may have lacked in formal education, she more than made up for with an impressive work ethic, and an astute business acumen. She built an entrepreneurial empire during an era when opportunities for women were often limited and always hard fought. Styled and coiffed with coordinating outfit, heels, and handbag, Grandma prepared herself daily for business appointments, outings to her properties, and errands. If she was having an *at home* day, she'd dress down. There'd be no heels, but house shoes.

Fortunately for Grandma, two of her three children and their families lived relatively close by her. This proximity allowed for frequent visits. Not so fortunately, her middle child and family were stationed with the military overseas. This year though, they were able to obtain leave to travel back to the United States for the holidays.

Grandma had nine grandchildren. There were the three cousins that we'd be driving to later Christmas Day, and the two cousins who lived on another continent. My brother, two sisters, and myself were the youngest of the group and filled out the rest of the nine tic-tac-toe squares.

As usual, there had been a bit of sibling drama, so we were running late this particular Christmas Day. We finally hurried out the door, loaded into our old Pontiac, and were on our way to my aunt and uncle's. Their home was a half hour drive past acres and acres of citrus trees and miles of cactus-dotted Arizona desert. These were all interesting enough to look at from the perspective of the back seat for perhaps the first five minutes of the journey.

When you're a kid, thirty minutes can seem like forever. Factor in Christmas Day excitement and sensory overload from the morning's earlier activities, and we were practically—no, actually—bouncing on the car's bench seat in anticipation. We were excited for the wonders awaiting us at this family gathering. There would be an abundance of food, laughter, and cousins.

I considered my aunt and uncle rich. They had a large home with wall-to-wall carpeting, a dishwasher, and air conditioning. There were doors and rooms in the home that we were allowed to enter and others that were off limits. They had nice things that we were to be careful around. Their yard was large, lush, green, and landscaped. In addition to the decorative plants that I couldn't name, they had pecan trees and a citrus orchard on their property.

Grandma lived a quick ten minutes from my aunt and uncle, so she was already there when we arrived. In all likelihood we tumbled out of the car slightly disheveled, but Grandma seemed not to notice our less-than-pristine appearance. At our entrance, hugs and such exclamations as, *My how you've all grown*, from our assorted adult relatives were exchanged. Greetings out of the way, we were then free within the previously noted parameters above, to explore.

As we ran out and about, and probably inadvertently slammed a door or two, Grandma settled into the sectional in my aunt and uncle's spacious, well-appointed living room. From that vantage point she could survey the holiday decorations around her, smell the tantalizing aromas coming from the kitchen, and also take part in grown-up conversations. Surprisingly for someone that seemed to rarely sit still, this would be Grandma's primary base of operations for the majority of the day and into the evening.

We children, young and not so young, scurried about the house and in and out of the living room. We frequently trooped to where Grandma was comfortably ensconced. Enchanted, she would exclaim her pleasure at seeing us, beam with delight, and gather us in. She was the hub in our wheel and we were the spokes. We radiated back to her, attracted by the love and sincere interest she emanated.

Grandma's face shone with joy that day. Eyes crinkling and alight with happiness, she seemed to be continuously smiling. I understood without fully comprehending that her glory and her greatest gifts were not in her business successes, but these precious moments invested with her family. I might not have been able to express that in words as a child, but I could feel it, and was drawn to her unconditional acceptance and caring.

My mind marks that Christmas past vividly and with a particular poignancy. To have us all collected under one roof happened infrequently. There would be even fewer occasions in the future when that occurred. Time gave my grandmother the gift of having her family gathered together to celebrate the birth of the Holy Child and to celebrate each other. She was filled and fulfilled.

The most valuable inheritance I received from my grandmother was not the funds that she left me, but her legacy of genuine love and support. I strive to emulate her example.

Hard to Save

By L. P. Masters

Well. There is nothing else to do, I suppose. I hang the wreath on the front door, then step back and look at it, despite the fact that I'm about to freeze to death. Literally. I've got a pair of socks on, my sweats, and an old T-shirt. The wreath looks beautiful. Even if it will be the death of me.

I'd told myself I would only be out here a moment; this would be fast. No need to put on all the coats and hats I've been burdened with all winter long.

If only I'd told myself to make sure I unlocked the handle before I stepped outside.

I knew what I'd done the moment the door shut. And I'd gone through all the arguing with myself already. So instead of yelling at myself any more, I decide to hang the wreath.

But now what? I frown and rub my hands over my arms, looking out at the street. Snow is falling beyond the cover of my porch. There's no point in ringing my doorbell. The bells would only make my dog, Stacie, bark like crazy. No one else is home. I'd planned to surprise my roommate, Evie, by setting up the Nativity by myself, and even hanging tinsel on the tree, because I know she likes it, but she thinks it is a tedious job. Everything looks perfect inside. And the wreath is hung on the door.

And now Evie might come home to a popsicle version of me. I blow into my hands and then try the handle one more time. Not sure why. It's obviously locked.

I check all my pockets again, hopelessly. I already know there's no key, and even my phone isn't on me. I left it inside, playing Christmas music at top volume.

I tap my freezing fingers on my leg and turn back around, looking out at the street. It's the weekend before Christmas, and I already know that half my neighbors are on vacation. Judging by the empty driveways and the darkened windows, the other half of my neighbors are at a party or something.

But there is one house with lights on inside. I groan.

Evie and I call the guy across the street Creepy Tom. I don't know how much I like the idea of going to his place as a woman in distress.

But I am in distress. I have to come to terms with that fact. What I haven't come to terms with, is the need to talk to Tom.

I don't want to have to spend a single minute more than is necessary in Tom's house. So I need a strategy before I even go over there to knock. I'll ask to use his phone, and then I'll call Evie.

What is her number?

She's speed dial number 3 in my phone, but that won't help much. I, of course, don't have my phone.

I could call my mom. I still have her number memorized, even though it's been years since I last talked to her. And how would that even help? She lives in Florida, and she wouldn't have Evie's number.

I grimace with frustration and pull my hair. A breeze picks up and blows across me and I drop my hair to wrap my arms around myself again. I'm shivering now, and my teeth are chattering. I really could freeze to death. I have no choice but to go over to Creepy Tom's.

I take a breath, take one step, and then stop.

A car is driving slowly down the road. I decide to wait for it to pass. I want to be able to run straight across and not have to wait at the curb with my socks in the snow.

It's a black car with tinted windows. And yes, the roads are slippery, but it seems like the car is driving much more slowly than is necessary. I tap my foot, waiting impatiently for the car to pass, but it slows even more, and then eventually comes to a stop in front of my driveway.

Great! Now there is a strange, dark car between me and Creepy Tom's house. And I'm still locked out.

The tinted window rolls down and a man leans across the passenger seat. "Are you okay?"

"I'm fine!" I reply, letting go of my death grip around my arms to give a quick wave. I hear the sound of a dog barking, but I figure it's just Stacie in the house, wondering who I'm talking to.

The guy looks forward through his windshield for a moment, and then back at me. "Do you need some help?"

Help getting murdered by a stranger? Nope. "No. I'm fine. Thank you."

He sits there for a moment and doesn't go anywhere. And then I hear barking again. It's not Stacie. A dog jumps over the back seat into the passenger seat and sticks its head out the windows, barking with a big doggie grin on its face. I can see a shaggy brown tail wagging behind it.

"Charlie. Get in the back!" the guy says. Then he pushes the dog back against the seat and looks out at me again. "Are you locked out?"

I frown and then nod as another shiver runs through me. I don't trust my voice to speak without shaking.

"Do you need me to give you a ride somewhere?"

"No. No, thank you. I'm fine."

Charlie starts barking again, and now Stacie is barking inside the house, and before I know it, the dog jumps out the open passenger window and rushes up the stairs to my porch.

His tail is going a mile a minute, and he smacks me on the thigh with it several times. I can't help but laugh as I kneel down and pet him. His fur is warm, and I cuddle into him, adoring the touch of heat I get. The man is yelling at him from the car. "Charlie! Get back here, you mutt!"

The car goes into park and the door opens. The man comes up on my porch. "I'm so sorry," he says, grabbing Charlie by the collar and pulling him away from me, stealing what little heat I'm getting from the dog. I stand up again, wrap my arms around myself.

The man looks me up and down and then he takes his black leather jacket off and wraps it around my shoulders. He's still wearing long sleeves, but it's got to be cold for him.

"What are you doing?" I demand, but I pull the coat tight around me.

"How long have you been out here?" he asks. He steps past me and checks the handle on my front door. Stacie barks, but of course, the door doesn't open. Charlie cuddles against my legs, and I like the warmth.

"I don't know. A few minutes."

"What's your plan?"

I stare at him. My mouth opens slightly but then I think. *I was planning to make my way over to Creepy Tom's.* Finally my shoulders fall and I drop my head. "I don't know," I say. "I don't really have a very good plan."

The man looks out towards his car on the street, then he looks back at me, then at the wreath on my door. He closes his eyes and rubs at his forehead. I can't deny that he's attractive, with dark hair that has a streak of gray in the sideburns, and a pair of square-rimmed glasses.

"Can I call someone for you?"

I shake my head. "I don't know my roommate's phone number."

"You got any family in town?"

I shake my head again and clench my jaw to keep my teeth from chattering. His coat is helping, but my feet feel like ice blocks.

"You don't make this easy."

"Well. Nothing worth it is easy."

Why on *earth* did I just say that?

He looks at me for a few seconds then stretches his hand out towards me. "I'm Anthony."

"Lila," I say, and shake his hand.

His skin is warm, and he winces when he feels mine. "You are freezing!"

I know I shouldn't cry, but all of a sudden I can't help it, and I burst out in tears. I bury my face in my freezing hands. "This is not how I wanted tonight to go!"

Anthony puts a hand on my shoulder and I gain control of myself pretty quickly. He looks towards the car. "You won't take a ride from me?"

Mom's voice yells in my ears. "Never accept a ride from a stranger!" I'm 47 now. I should be old enough to make my own choices, but I still can't get over the instructions that she pounded into my brain every day until I was eighteen.

I shake my head.

"Do you have a back door, or a window you might have left unlocked?"

"I doubt it." Evie and I are both pretty good about locking things up.

A wind picks up and blows across the porch again. I exhale sharply, and now I can't stop my teeth from chattering.

Anthony sighs loudly and then says, "Call the cops on me for kidnapping you, but you're not staying here a minute longer!"

"Wha..."

He picks me up in his arms and starts down the stairs. "Charlie, come on!"

"What are you doing?" I demand. "Where are you taking me?"

"Rosauers," he says. "Or whatever store is still open tonight. You're going somewhere warm right now!"

He leans down, with me still in his arms, and opens the passenger door. The window is still rolled down from when he was talking to me. He sets me on the leather seat. It has a seat heater on, and the heater is running full blast inside the car. My cheeks and fingers and toes all tingle in the heat and it feels amazing.

Anthony shuts the door, then opens the back door and ushers Charlie in. I notice the back seat has a towel over it, to protect from the dog's soggy paws. Anthony comes around to the driver's side and gets in. He looks at me, and must see the utter terror on my face. He stretches his lips tight and says, "Look, I'm not actually kidnapping you, but you can't stay here, and you know it, right?"

I nod, and a few tears tumble from my eyes again.

"What can I do to help you feel more comfortable with this? Do you want to see my ID? Send a picture of it to someone who's phone number you do know?"

I think about that. I could send a text to Mom, let her know what's going on. Let her know if I don't call her by 9 when Evie gets home that she should call the cops. But I know Mom. She'll call the cops before Anthony could even put his car in drive. And the FBI, and the CIA. Not really. But Mom is an overreacter.

I sigh and look back at my house. Stacie is looking out the window, her tail whacking the curtains. "Do you have paper and a pen?"

"Yes."

"Let me write a note to my roommate. I can give her your phone number, and she can come pick me up when she gets off work."

Anthony nods. He reaches across and opens the glove compartment. It's incredibly organized, nothing at all like my own glove compartment. He hands me a notebook and pen and I start to write. I tell Evie everything about Anthony, even his birthdate and his license plate number. I ask him to get out and take a picture of the plate so I know it's right.

When I figure I have done everything in my power to make sure I don't get kidnapped, I hand the note to Anthony and he walks it up to my porch, sliding it into the crack between the frame and the door.

Charlie puts his head over the back of my seat and I pat him gently, watching Anthony come back from my porch. I can see the note on the door. I guess I've done my best.

Anthony gets in and puts the car in drive. My stomach knots up, and we travel the whole way there in silence. He drives straight to Rosauers. He doesn't have navigation on his phone, and he doesn't ask me for directions, so he must be familiar with the neighborhood.

When we get to the store, I relax a little. He turns the car off and comes around to my door, lifting me out like I'm weightless... Which I'm not! I definitely have a few extra pounds on me that I wouldn't mind losing. But I also don't mind eating all the Christmas cookies we get at work, so I don't expect the pounds to come off anytime soon.

Thankfully, Rosauers has an automatic opening door. Anthony puts me down on the ground as soon as we're inside, and he looks around. "There's a little cafe type of thing around here somewhere, and a fireplace. Let's go find it."

I nod. I'm still wearing his coat, and now I realize that it smells like aftershave. It's a sharp scent, but I rather like it.

We find the fireplace and I sit right in front of it, warming my hands just like I did in front of his vents in his car.

"Is Charlie going to be okay out in the car?" I ask.

"I'm sure Charlie is fine."

I take a deep breath and finally feel safe for the first time since the moment I realized the door was locked. "Thank you," I say to him.

Anthony smiles. "You're welcome. I will admit, though, you're a hard woman to save."

"That's because I hate to admit that I need saving." I pause and look into the fake flames, glad that at least the heat is real. "But I really did need saving tonight."

"You really had no plans for what you were going to do?"

"Well, I was considering knocking on the neighbor's door, but... He's the kind of guy you only talk to if you have no other choice."

Anthony chuckles.

"By the way," I say. "What were you doing driving down my street anyway?"

"Heading home. I decided to leave my sister's party early."

"Oh." I want to ask where he lives, and then realize that might be creepy. Instead I ask, "Where does your sister live?" And then wonder if that's really any better.

"In the Valley."

"Well, I guess I'm grateful you decided to leave early."

"I am, too."

I smile at him. "Why is that?"

He shrugs, then looks at me, his eyes bright. "I guess... Because you look so good in my jacket."

I pull it close around me and glance down. I can feel my face flushing, but I tell myself it's just because the fire is finally starting to warm me up.

Anthony looks around. "Are you hungry?"

I'm famished, but I don't want to be any more of a burden than I already am. "No. I'm fine."

"Uh huh." He just looks at me, but his eyes are laughing. "Just like you were fine standing on your porch in a T-shirt."

My eyes drift to the floor and I don't say anything.

"Well, I'm going to get some hot chicken before the deli closes. I'll grab a few extra drumsticks just in case you change your mind."

He walks away, and I can't help but smile. I am grateful he saved me, and I feel guilty for making him buy me dinner, but I really am starving.

He comes back a few minutes later with a giant box of food. Chicken, potatoes, broccoli salad, and rolls.

For the next hour we sit in front of the big fireplace sharing the food and chatting about whatever comes to mind. I almost forget that Anthony is a complete stranger. I share things with him that I would never have considered sharing with someone like Creepy Tom.

When his phone rings, I catch my breath. I glance at the clock on the wall and realize it's just past nine. I look at the screen of his phone and see that the call is coming in from a local number, but it's not saved to his phone.

"Hello?"

"Is Lila there?" Evie's voice sounds panicked. I can hear her from where I'm sitting next to him.

"Yeah. Here she is."

I take his phone. "Hi, Evie."

"Are you safe?"

"Yes."

Evie sighs, and then she pauses for a moment. "What happened?"

"Uh. It's a long story. I'll have to tell you about it later. Could you come pick me up?"

"Of course! Where are you?"

"I'm at the Rosauers just down the hill."

"I'll be there in five minutes."

I want to tell her "Take your time," but she has already hung up. I look down at Anthony's phone for a moment, and then hand it back to him. "Evie's on her way."

Anthony looks sincerely disappointed, just like I feel.

"Thank you again," I say.

"Anytime," he says, and then catches himself.

I grin. "Anytime I lock myself out of my house, you'll come to the rescue?"

"Hey, that rescue was hard, I'll tell you that!"

I laugh and tilt my head back as I do it. "Well, I'll give you that."

He stares at me for a little while. And then he asks, "Will you give me something else?"

Confused, I ask, "What?"

"Your phone number? So I can call it, after you put it back in your pocket and agree to leave it there *at all times*."

I chuckle, and think about that. Do I want him having my phone number? But the moment I ask myself that question, the answer comes full force. Yes!

I can't tell him yes that quickly, though. Not after how hard I said no to him saving me. I shrug. "I don't know. I guess we will have to see if Charlie and Stacie get along. And I don't want you dropping by without texting or calling me first. So I suppose I ought to give you my number."

He hands me his phone again, with the "add new contact" screen already up.

I start typing in my phone number, but don't get all the way through it before his phone starts to ring. It's that same number again. It must be Evie. I answer it. "Hello?"

"Lila. I'm here. Come out to the parking lot."

"I'll be right out." I hand him the phone back and then do something absolutely crazy, something I wouldn't have ever considered doing with any stranger in my life. I give him a hug. "Thank you so much."

He still holds me tight and says near my ear, "You're welcome, Lila. I'm glad I saw you there."

He doesn't let me go right away. And I don't let him go either. There's a weird part of me that doesn't want to. I could stand here in this embrace for another hour.

And then I snap out of it and realize I need to get out to the parking lot and meet Evie. I let go and pull away, and start to walk. He follows me.

"I have to go," I say.

"I know. And I have to help you," he replies. "Unless you want to walk across the parking lot in your socks."

I look down. I have almost forgotten I'm only wearing socks. Then I see that I still have his jacket on, and I start to take it off. He puts his hand on my back. "Keep it. I'll pick it up when Charlie and Stacie meet."

"Thanks." I didn't really want to give it back to him anyway.

We get to the automatic doors and I walk to the very edge, stopping before I have to step out into the cold. "You ready?" he asks. A little gentler than the first time he swept me up into his arms.

"Yeah," I say. Even though I want to say no. I don't want this night to end. I don't want our conversation to end. "I had a great time."

"Me, too." Anthony swings me into his arms and steps out into the parking lot. It's snowing again, and I see Evie's car just sitting there in the crosswalk. She's not parked, she's just waiting.

She reaches across the front seat, opening the passenger side door so Anthony doesn't have to bend down and do it himself. He sets me in the seat. It's not a heated seat like his was, but the heater is warm.

"I'm not carrying you up the stairs to our house," Evie says.

"I can help," Anthony offers.

"No, thank you," Evie responds before I have a moment to say anything. "I'll grab her shoes from the house and bring them out to her. You may not have noticed, but she is actually capable of walking."

Anthony smiles. "I noticed." He looks at me. "Bye, Lila."

"Bye."

He closes my door softly. Evie screeches out of the parking lot. "Are you crazy?" she asks. "Letting some random guy take you somewhere?"

I look over at her. "Would you have preferred me to freeze to death?"

She rolls her eyes as if I'm being dramatic, but I'm not. I really would have frozen to death. "My other option could have been to go over and ask Creepy Tom for help. I suppose that would have been so much safer, huh?"

"Ugh! No! Don't ever talk to Creepy Tom if you can help it. Especially when you have no chance of getting away." She rubs her eyes tiredly. "I'm sorry. I guess I'm overreacting a little. I just was super worried about you."

I smile and nod. I had been worried when I first met Anthony. But after spending time with him, not so much.

It's quiet in the car the rest of the way home. All I can think about is Anthony and the conversations we had. We come around the corner and Evie drives down our street, pulling into the driveway. Then she glances at me and shakes her head with a smile on her face. "Anyway. The Nativity and the wreath look nice."

I smile back. "I'm glad you like them."

HOME FOR CHRISTMAS

BY VICTORIA COLVER

Part 1: Clive
Christmas, 1934

Clive looked over his family's farm and wondered if the harvest would be enough to keep them afloat. Rust had crippled their wheat, the oats had been cut green and the barley was low in weight. Not only did they have accounts in town that needed to be paid but they were behind on both their taxes and the loan on the farm. The weight fell heavy on his shoulders.

He squinted at a growing speck in the distance. It was his father striding towards him. He came with news from town: paying work up North.

"But who will run the farm?"

"Your brother will manage. Sixteen is old enough and there won't be a farm if you don't take this job. We can't turn our backs on good money."

"I've never been a teacher."

"You'll learn. It's already settled. The missionary in charge of the school heads back north tomorrow. You'll go with him."

Tomorrow? Clive turned away from his father's lined face to the train track that ran through the field. That train had driven through his field six days a week for as long as he had been alive but he had never ridden it. Tomorrow all that would change. He'd be on that train and on his way up to northern Canada. It was cold and lonely up there. Like being on an island. He supposed that was why his destination had been named Island Lake.

He would miss the farm and the fields. But Father was right. He couldn't afford to turn his back on good money. Not when work was so scarce and the cost of living so high.

The next day Clive took the train north with the missionary. After the train he took a steamship even further north and after that a floatplane. When Clive finally arrived at Island Lake, he found a log cabin waiting for him. It was small but adequate for a man living by himself. A pair of snowshoes was tacked to the outer wall. There was a small garden to the side that had already been planted. A farming man, he could tell from a distance what the plants were. There was only one type. It was a good thing he liked potatoes.

He looked around for more buildings—the school, the students' houses—but he could see none. The only other thing he could see aside from his own cabin was a canoe that rested on the shore.

Clive turned to the missionary who had accompanied him.

"School's on the other side of the lake. Take that there canoe across and ring the bell when you get there."

"But where are the children?" A loon's lonely call echoed across the lake. The sound seemed to make the lake and its surroundings even emptier.

"Just ring the bell. They'll come." Then he clapped Clive on the back and left.

Clive stood on the dock looking after him. The engines of the float plane whirred and then faded into the distance. He stood there and listened until he could no longer hear them. The silence was absolute.

The next morning Clive climbed into the canoe, paddled across the lake and rang the bell. Before he knew it, he had a classroom filled with children. He didn't know where the children came from, he just rang the bell and they had come running. He looked at them with their tan skin, dark hair and even darker eyes. They stared back at him, silent and expectant. The fields didn't look back at him at home. He took a deep breath and began with the alphabet.

Back and forth he paddled his canoe each day. Each day was colder than the last. When the lake froze over, he took the snowshoes off the wall, fastened them to his feet and walked across. He carried a long stick to tap the ice ahead of him, testing its strength as he went. If he fell through there would be no rescue.

Everyday the children came running when Clive rang the bell and every day he returned to his cabin alone. At first he found it peaceful but soon the quiet became oppressive. His only friend was the wind that made his cabin shudder.

One day when winter had set in, the silence and loneliness felt heavier than usual. Clive finished his dinner of boiled potatoes and listened to the wind howl and buffet the walls. He moved closer to the fire holding the only picture he'd been able to bring with him. It was a picture of him and his younger brother posing with the rest of the threshing crew at the previous year's harvest.

He cracked a small smile. It had been such a great day. They'd been threshing since before sun up and they were hot and dusty. After the picture had been taken, he'd thrown Denny in the stock pond and then jumped in after him. An ache started in his chest and spread until it reached his eyes. Clive swiped roughly at the tears and shook his head to think it was the land he thought he'd miss most.

He glanced at the calendar hanging on the wall. December 21. Four days until Christmas. The supply plane would arrive tomorrow. He hoped there might be a letter from home packed in with the tins of food. How he wished he could be with his family, even just for one day. He threw another log on the fire and then poked it as he made a plan.

The next day, Clive put on his snow shoes and went to meet the supply plane as usual only this time he took a rucksack and climbed aboard. The supply plane took him to where he could catch a steamboat south and after that the train.

When he stepped wearily from the train, he had been traveling for three days. The platform was empty. No one was waiting for him. He hadn't had time to write and tell his family he was coming. The moon lit his path as he began the eight-mile walk home along frozen country roads.

Christmas morning had just begun to spread its cheery pink light over the horizon when Clive finally made it home. He opened the front door to find his younger brother seated on the stairs tying his boots for chores. Denny blinked and then yelled, "Ma! Clive's home!" He tripped over his laces to reach his brother.

Ma stuck her head out from the kitchen, still stirring the batter for breakfast and not stopping until she saw him with her own eyes. Batter slopped onto the counter as the bowl hit it with a clang and she rushed to Clive. Her arms wrapped around him and she shook, her face buried in his shoulder.

Father entered and placed a solid hand on Clive's shoulder. There was squealing and a pattering of bare feet as his three little sisters made their way down the stairs in their nightgowns. A warmth started in Clive's chest and spread to his eyes. This time he didn't wipe the tears away. He held his family and cried, grateful to be home even if it was only for a day. There would be no gifts to open and their breakfast would be simple but it was the happiest Christmas Clive would ever have.

Part 2: Dorothy
Christmas, WWII

Chapter 1, 1941

"Let's run home," Dorothy called to her sister Afton. The chill night air bit at her cheeks as they exited the Christmas Eve dance but she didn't care. Somehow after hours of dancing she still had energy she needed to burn.

Sleigh bells and laughter rang through the stillness of snow covered fields as they ran and slid clinging to the back of the sleigh with Ruth, the oldest sister, at the reins. When at last they reached the farm, Dorothy's cheeks were flushed from the exertion and she was warmed through. Ruth, however, was half frozen and rushed into the farmhouse while the younger girls cared for the horse and sleigh.

"Who was that soldier you were dancing with tonight?" The harness clinked as Afton hefted it onto its hook.

Dorothy flushed, and this time not from the cold.

"Which soldier?" She didn't look up. She grabbed the brush and began grooming the horse.

Afton would not be put off. "You know exactly who I'm talking about Dorothy, now spill."

Dorothy smiled at the horse's back, avoiding her gaze, and kept on brushing. Afton came and stood on the other side of the horse.

"What's his name?"

"Clive," she whispered.

"And who is he?"

How could she describe him? Handsome. Not too tall but with strong shoulders. Stormy blue eyes. A young farmer from Manitoba stationed here in Cardston with the Canadian military. He had been fortunate not to be sent overseas with the other young men she'd danced with in recent years. So many of whom she'd never dance with again. Is that what Afton wanted to hear?

Or did she want to hear that before he'd enlisted with the military he'd been a teacher way up in northern Canada. A place so isolated it was called an island, even though it was surrounded by land. Dorothy thought of him up there alone and wondered if he might go back there when the war was over—if she might go with him.

"He asked me to marry him."

"He didn't!" Afton gasped. "But you've only just met!"

It was true. A month's worth of weekend serviceman's balls wasn't much but it felt as if they'd known each other for years.

"Dorothy," he'd whispered in her ear as they swayed to the music, "I know I'm a fool for saying this but dancing here with you, I feel as though I'm on my farm again, standing on the back forty." He laughed softly and pulled her closer. "I'll be darned if I can't see the Manitoba prairie stretching for miles in your eyes."

A silly thing to say—that he saw the prairie in her eyes. Perhaps it was simply because her eyes were the color of a rich soil ready for planting. But Dorothy had felt her heart swell at those words. What he had described was his home. He saw his home in her eyes. She was a practical girl but she couldn't think of anything more romantic.

Dorothy pulled the brush across the horse's back over and over until Afton swatted at her. "You'll brush the horse bald if you keep going in the same spot. Now tell me, what did you say?"

"Well," Dorothy started slowly, "Of course I couldn't say yes. As you said, we've only just met."

Afton crossed her arms and furrowed her brow. "But what did you want to say?"

If she were a few years older, say twenty, and she'd known him a little longer, what would she have said? She knew what she wanted to say but she tucked that into her heart.

"I told him I'd write to him."

"And what about Mary?"

Mary? Oh yes. Dorothy hadn't forgotten about her plans to visit her sister Mary. She bit her lip. She considered what might happen if she put off going to Mary's—stuck around, went to a few more dances, got to know a certain soldier a little better. How long would he be stationed in Cardston? Long enough for her to reconsider his offer? Long enough for him to offer again?

"I can write to him from Mary's. The post won't stop just because I've moved to a different address."

"But Mary's all the way down in the States! And what if you meet another fellow there?"

"And what if I do? I've only agreed to write to Clive. Nothing more. There's no promise I'd be breaking." Dorothy said the words but she felt in her heart that it was unlikely she'd meet someone else. No one else could possibly tell her that they saw the Manitoba prairie in her eyes.

"What did Mother say when you told her?"

"Told her what?"

"About going to live with Mary."

Dorothy paused as she put the brush away. She still hadn't talked to Mother about her plans to visit Mary but she intended to go regardless of what Mother said.

"I haven't told her."

"You'd better tell her soon. The train leaves in two days and it won't wait for her to finish giving you the silent treatment so you can say a proper goodbye."

Afton opened the barn door and frigid air engulfed them. Dorothy shivered, the warmth from her run having worn off. She pulled her coat tighter around her neck as the girls made their way to the farmhouse. Stars pierced the inky sky, the Milky Way clearly visible above them. Ribbons of pink and green light undulated in a strange dance along the horizon. Over and over they moved apart and then collided as though they belonged together.

Chapter 2

Dorothy laid on her bed and stared into the darkness.

What would Mother say when she told her she wanted to go live with Mary? And when she told her that the reason was so she could go to school? Surely Mother would want her to be happy. But would she want her to be happy more than she needed Dorothy's income from the hairdresser's shop? Her wages alone had bought all the Christmas presents, and that didn't include the new glasses she'd ordered for her little brother earlier that year.

What if she stayed home? That would make Mother happy and she could get to know Clive better. A fluttering sensation tickled in her belly. It wasn't the worst outcome she could think of. But what if Clive offered again and Dorothy said yes like she knew she would? She would leave home anyway and take her money with her. It was simply something Mother would have to face. If Dorothy was to live her own life, her mother would have to make ends meet without her.

"Afton?"

A coyote yipped in the distance. Dorothy sighed and rolled to face the wall. She wished that Afton was awake to talk things through. Talking to her sister always made her problems seem smaller. She squeezed her eyes shut and willed herself to sleep.

The talk with Mother went about as well as she thought it would. Mother was upset and worried about how they would continue to pay for the farm without her wages but Dorothy stood her ground.

"I want more than to curl another woman's hair for the rest of my life."

"The hairdresser's is good work. There's no sense in chasing a silly dream when you've got bread and butter right in front of you."

"I want to learn. I want to do something important."

Mother rose from the table and moved to stand at the sink. "Stuff and nonsense, child."

"I'm not a child." Dorothy's words were quiet and firm.

Her mother picked up a scrub brush but did not acknowledge Dorothy's words. Had Mother not heard her? She'd heard her alright. It was her way of telling Dorothy that the conversation was over.

Dorothy did not move.

"Whether I go off to school or find a young man to marry, I will leave this farm."

Her mother's head snapped up. "You found someone?"

Dorothy flushed. She hadn't meant to say that. "I mean to live with Mary whether you approve or not. I leave tomorrow."

Her mother scrubbed the casserole dish with added vigor.

"Please, don't make me leave like this."

Dorothy jumped as the casserole dish clattered into the sink. Her mother turned to face her. Dorothy held her breath. "You've neither the brains nor the looks. You'll be back at the hairdresser's before the month's out. And you'll be sorry you ever left."

It was not how she wanted to leave. It was a long distance there and back. If something were to happen while she was away, there'd be no making it home in time to say goodbye. But her mother's words had lit a fire in her. Maybe it was true that she didn't have the brains or the looks. But she would go to school and she would succeed. If there was anything she knew for certain, it was that she wanted to go to school now more than ever.

Dorothy set her suitcase down on the train station platform and checked her ticket. There was only one platform so she didn't have to worry about getting on the wrong train but she'd never left home before and checking the train number and departure time seemed like a way to ease her nerves.

Loud voices and heavy footfalls caught Dorothy's attention as a group of soldiers walked past her. Dorothy craned her neck searching for a set of broad shoulders and steel blue eyes. When she didn't find them, she picked up her suitcase and held it in front of her, tapping the handle with her thumbs. She set it down and opened her handbag and checked for the pen and paper she'd stashed inside.

She would prove her mother wrong even if it meant that some things would have to wait.

Chapter 3, 1942

Dorothy ran into the house and let the screen door slam behind her. She tore open the envelope as she ran upstairs to her room. She grabbed a blanket from the end of the bed and wrapped it around her shoulders before flopping onto the bed to read her letter.

She had been in the States with her sister for a year now. She and Clive had exchanged letters every week since then. He'd been surprised and sad to hear of her departure but he was pleased to hear that she was happy. She had begun work at the hospital with Mary and started training to be a nurse's aide. The other nurses were happy to have her help and eager to teach her. She felt a thrill in her chest every time she was able to help someone at the hospital. She felt needed. She felt important. And for once in her life, she felt smart.

Clive's letter began the usual way telling her how much he missed her but instead of telling some antics of the other soldiers or something he had done that week, he wrote that he had received orders. Dorothy clutched at her blanket, a sickening feeling in her belly. He was to be transferred to England and would be leaving the next day. Dorothy looked at the date at the top of the letter. He had already left and was on his way.

She thought of the many friends who had gone overseas to fight the war. Afton had written recently that they'd received word that a school chum had been shot and killed. He was not the only one who'd not be coming home.

The thought of Clive leaving... she couldn't bear it. If only she hadn't been so stubborn and stayed. Perhaps things would be different. Then her good sense took hold of her. Yes, perhaps things would have been different.

Perhaps you'd be an eighteen-year-old widow with a baby on the way. Foolish girl. It was her mother's voice she heard in her head now.

Dorothy sobbed for the better part of an hour. When she could finally control her emotions she moved to her writing desk. Her pen hovered above the paper but she couldn't write a single word. How could she continue writing to Clive, growing fonder with each heartfelt letter, only to have to say goodbye? Or worse, to not be able to say goodbye? It was best to do it now then to not be able to at all. She lay back down on her bed and cried herself to sleep.

Chapter 4

Dear Dorothy,

I haven't heard from you for some time but I suppose the mail is slow in crossing the pond, as they say here. I miss you terribly. I think of that night we spent dancing together often. I would give anything to be back home with you in my arms.

I had some leave recently and spent it visiting family. My mother still has family living in England and they were happy to hear news of her relations. I was happy to sleep in a real bed for a change. Staying in their home was a real treat. Camp cots and barracks have grown tiresome and I've found myself thinking of home an awful lot. And you, of course.

Please write.

Clive

Chapter 5, 1946

Dorothy smoothed the skirt of her black dress as Mary's husband entered the small kitchen. He was dressed in a dark suit but nothing about him looked put together. He drew a weary hand over his face. "I–I can't stay here."

"But where will you go? What about Carolyn?" Dorothy thought of the little niece she'd often cared for and grown so attached to.

Melvin looked towards the stairs that led to the nursery where she was napping. "I'm taking Carolyn with me to my mother's. List the house in the local newspaper. As soon as you've arranged for the sale you can go home."

Dorothy traced the grain of the oak table, blinking back tears as she nodded her understanding. Mary's life had been taken so abruptly. The house was nothing but a reminder of what they'd lost. She understood their grief as if it were her own. It *was* her own.

But unlike Melvin, Dorothy was unsure of where to go. What home was there for her now? She might stay in Provo, find another place to live, but with the war over and the nurses returning home, she also found herself without work. It seemed as quickly as she'd made a new home for herself that home had disappeared.

Perhaps, like Melvin, she might also return to her mother's home? She shook her head. Not with how she had left, and not with the dreams she still had for herself.

And what about the proposal of marriage she had received five years earlier? It felt like a lifetime ago, so much had happened since that day. A fresh ache clenched at her heart. She didn't know what had become of Clive. She had stopped writing to him when he had been sent overseas. She wanted to save herself the heartache of grieving his death but she'd grieved his loss all the same.

There was a knock at the door. It was the neighbor with a letter for Dorothy.

"We received this in our mail. Seems it was meant for you."

She pocketed the letter. She couldn't read another card bearing condolences. She was overwhelmed with grief. It was too much to bear on her own and she felt so very alone.

"Where to?" The ticket master tapped his fingers impatiently.

Dorothy stared at the destination board in indecision. *Where to?* It was days away from Christmas and she wanted nothing more than to be home. But having sold Mary and Melvin's house, where was home exactly?

Dorothy found herself at a crossroads, not knowing which path to take. Knowing that each path led to a different destination with entirely different views—that the path she chose might be one she'd walk for the rest of her life.

She had dressed in her black dress for travel and as she vacillated between the various destinations she felt something in her pocket. It was the letter that had been delivered after Mary's funeral. She had forgotten to open it. She pulled it out and recognized the writing immediately. The ticket master was waiting and a queue was beginning to form behind her. She opened the letter anyway. A spark of hope flickered in her heart as she read the words that told of a long-awaited homecoming.

"Where to?" the ticket master asked again. Dorothy bit her lip as she clutched the bit of paper to her chest and stepped forward.

Suitcase in one hand and the letter in the other, Dorothy stepped from the train onto the platform. She'd never seen such a flat, barren landscape as the one that was before her now. She couldn't see the rich soil she'd heard so much about but she knew it was there, hidden underneath the snow. She breathed in the crisp winter air and looked around her, hoping her telegram had arrived in time. Her hands shook nervously until her eyes came to rest on a set of strong shoulders and stormy blue eyes. A calm warmth rose in her chest and she knew she was home.

Part 3: Julianne
Christmas, 2024

Chapter 1

"What does love feel like, Auntie Julianne?"

I shift my eyes to look at my niece Adelynn through the mirror but I don't move a single facial muscle. I'm frozen in what's better known as *mascara face*. Mouth in an O and eyes open wide, I flit the brush over my lashes and grunt something that sounds like, "Ah-oh-no."

"You don't know? You mean you've never been in love?" Of course, she doesn't need any interpretation. Adelynn is ten and just like a little sister to me. She even looks like me with her long, sandy brown hair and dark eyes. She does a somersault upwards on my bed and lands with her back on my pillow and her feet on the wall.

"Never??" That's Shela, blonde pigtails flying as she jumps up and down on the other end of my bed. She's three going on thirteen. Her favorite word is *Never*.

"But how would you even know you're in love if you don't know what it feels like?" asks Savvy. She's standing beside me experimenting with festive shades of eyeshadow. One eye has a red lid with green brow bone and the other is the opposite. She's got feisty strawberry blonde hair and classic eight-year-old style to go with it.

"Add some gold." I hold out a compact to her and she reaches eagerly for it.

"You have ta kiss him ta know. Kiss him an' then the birds sing." Shela is an expert on matters of love.

I pull out my curling iron and tap it to see if it's hot enough. Out of nowhere, a three-year-old finger reaches to copy me and I catch it millimeters before it touches searing hot metal.

I turn to find Shela reaching over my shoulder. Her eyes are big like she thinks she's in trouble. "Only Auntie does that. Okay, cute stuff?" She nods then scurries back to the bed and hides under the covers.

"I'll curl your hair when I'm done with mine," I call to her. I'll win her back, no problem.

"Is Shela sleeping in here with us tonight?" Savvy crosses her arms and raises one golden eyebrow at me through the mirror. It's a Christmas tradition that all the nieces old enough to sleep away from their parents have a slumber party in Auntie Juju's room. It makes more room for other siblings plus it's really fun. I love having all the girls in my room; it makes me feel like the coolest aunt ever. Christmas wouldn't be the same without them.

"Her mom said she could so I'm okay with it."

"But she'll pee the bed!" Savvy whines.

Shela's now-fuzzy pigtailed head pops immediately out of the covers. "I never!"

"Mom!" she sobs as she makes her way towards the hall, "Savvy say I pee the bed and I never!"

Within seconds my sister Nora is leaning against my door frame, Shela wrapped around her ankles. "So you decided to go to the dance?"

"McKell practically begged me to go with her." I grab a section of hair and wrap it around my curling iron.

"Sounds like it'll be fun," she smiles and then hesitates. "And then we get you all to ourselves, right? We've got to get in as much sister time as we can before you leave again."

Knowing I've only got two weeks before I leave to start a master's program on the East Coast, I do want to be home. Just stepping inside the house and smelling Mom's cooking then sinking into a familiar chair, *my chair*, by the fire, I felt worries I didn't know I carried lift off my shoulders. Like I could finally relax and be myself. I hadn't realized how much hominess my dorm room lacked. Cinder block walls and a used twin bed just can't compete. It feels so good to be home, but how could I say no to McKell?

"I will give you every other second I am home. Promise. Besides, you guys spend the evening putting your kids down and then you go to bed early. There's not much I'll be missing out on."

"Are you going to wake us up when you get home?" Adelynn is still upside down. How has the blood not rushed to her head yet?

"Hopefully not."

"But we want to hear all about the dance!" Adelynn complains.

"I'll tell you everything in the morning," I assure her.

"Is that what you're going to wear?" Nora nods at my sweater. It's Mom's reindeer sweater with the multicolored bobbles hanging off of it.

"The theme is Tacky Christmas. I thought this was appropriate."

"Nice. Maybe don't tell Mom though. You might hurt her feelings if she finds out you think her favorite Christmas sweater is tacky."

"Oh, I forgot these." I slip on a pair of elf ears.

Nora laughs. "Don't go meeting anyone. It'll make moving to the East Coast really hard."

"I've been dreaming of becoming a pediatric nurse practitioner ever since I became an auntie when I was ten. I've got plans. I'm not going to meet someone."

Nora tweaks my elf ear. "Ditch the ears then. They make you irresistible."

I feel a small body climb onto my lap. "My turn, Auntie Juju?" Shela is all puppy eyes and sweetness. I smile to myself. I knew she'd be back.

Chapter 2

When I get to the dance, I'm surprised to see how many people are there. I guess a lot of college-age kids are home for the holidays. The music is loud and the gym has been decked out in true Tacky Christmas style. There are yard inflatables of all kinds along the edges of the gym: Snoopys, snow globes, Darth Vaders, penguins, Surf's Up Santa, Santa stuck in a chimney, even a Nativity is squashed in there. You name it, it's in there. It's a wonder we don't blow a circuit. I love it.

"C'mon," McKell grabs my arm. "Let's scope out the refreshment table before all the good stuff is gone."

"Didn't we come here to dance?" I say as she drags me to the long tables lining the far wall.

"The men will be here all night. The cookies will not."

She was right. There are lots of cookies from Rosauers and Yokes but only a few that are homemade and the homemade ones look delicious.

Darth Vader glares at me from behind the table as I try to choose between a sugar cookie bar and a chocolate peppermint sandwich cookie. I jump when a deep voice says, "I'd take them both. Just to be safe."

It's not Darth and it's not McKell. It's a guy who looks older than most of the guys here, but not in a bad way. He has wavy hair that's kind of messy-cute, and warm brown eyes. Like hot chocolate.

I smile as I pull them both, cookies, not his eyes, onto my plate. "Good idea. I'm Julianne, by the way."

"Rally." He grabs an oatmeal-looking cookie and adds it to my plate. "Don't forget one of these. Mom's secret recipe."

"You brought these?" Before he can answer, McKell is at my side and pulling me away.

"Hey!" I look back over my shoulder and give Rally an apologetic smile.

"Hey, nothing. I just saved you." McKell has one hand on my elbow and the other holding a plate piled high with treats.

"What do you mean? From him? He seemed super nice." I glance over my shoulder again. Rally has moved on to talk to some other people. He's cheerful and everyone in the group seems to really like him. He sees me looking and winks. My face flushes.

"Don't let Ralph deceive you," McKell leads me to some chairs lining the wall. "He comes to these activities pretending like he's all nice and friendly but in truth, he's on the prowl for a wife. All the girls know it and all the girls keep their distance."

I laugh off her comments. "News flash, Kell-Kell, all the boys here are on the prowl for a wife. That's why they're here and not at home playing video games."

"Well, those boys are okay. This one is not."

I look at her funny. "Kell-Kell, what is up with you? Did he break your heart or something?"

She shoves a cookie in her mouth and shakes her head while she swallows. "He's actually too old to be here. No one really knows how old he is. I think he might be close to forty."

I chance another look at him. There's no way he's older than my brother Henry. If I had to guess, I'd say he's only in his early thirties.

"Why did you call him Ralph? He said his name was Rally."

"Rally's short for Ralph. It's such an old man's name. I always call him by his real name so I don't forget how old he is."

I start to feel glad that I've been away at school. McKell was my best friend all growing up and we were both heartbroken when I went away to university and she stayed home to attend the community college. I was so excited to spend time with her tonight but now it seems like she's changed while I was away. She's not as fun as she used to be, or as nice.

"I don't think it's a bad thing that he's a bit older."

"Maybe," she nibbles another cookie. "But just think about it. Let's say you go on a date with him and you take him home afterwards and he meets your mom and you realize he's closer to your mom's age than yours and actually, he could date your mom if she were single and it wouldn't be that weird."

I freeze with a cookie midway to my mouth and just stare at McKell. I have no words.

A swing song comes on and Rally asks me to dance. I don't even look at McKell to see her reaction. He's super nice and I'm not afraid of him, even if he is as old as McKell says.

We twist and turn to the music. It feels amazing. I had been so focused on school I had forgotten how fun this could be. At the end, he dips me and before I can stop myself I let out a loud whoop.

A slow song starts and I'm about to head back to McKell when Rally catches my hand and asks me if I'll dance with him again. My cheeks flush a little and I nod.

"Where did you learn to swing so well?" I enunciate to be heard over the music.

"My mom," he smiles. Who could hate a guy who learns to dance from his mom?

"And did she make the cookie you put on my plate?"

"Nope. I did. But I used her secret recipe." Bakes and loves his mom. Nice combo.

"Well, I'm glad you did. It was delicious. I've never had an orange-flavored oatmeal cookie before."

"She makes them every year. They're my favorite. How about you? Did you bring anything?"

I feel a little embarrassed. "No, I wasn't planning on coming tonight." I start to tell him that I'm leaving for school on the East Coast after the holidays are over but for some reason I can't bring myself to say it.

Chapter 3

After the dance Rally and some other guys invite a bunch of girls over to their house to watch a movie. McKell rolls her eyes but I convince her to go. "C'mon, it'll be fun."

The guys' house is old and small. It feels especially small with a dozen adult bodies crammed into the front room. The girls pile onto two couches and the boys sprawl out on the floor.

Rally puts the movie on but then pauses it and blocks the screen with his body. "First person to guess the movie gets to hold the popcorn bowl."

He steps aside to reveal a dark screen with a few stars and two glowing clouds. It's obviously an older movie; the graphics are terrible and it looks like it'll be black and white.

The group seems stumped but I know exactly what we're watching. I watch it with my mom every year around this time. It's her favorite and definitely one of mine as well.

"It's a Wonderful Life," I whisper.

Rally points directly at me, surprise on his face. "Miss Julianne. That is correct. You have won yourself a popcorn bowl."

He hands it to me and then whacks the guy sitting on the ground in front of me so that he can take that spot himself.

Some of the others text or giggle through the movie but not me. I enjoy every second of it. And I can't help but cry when the town saves George and everyone sings Auld Lang Syne at the end.

The screen goes dark and someone switches on Mario Cart. I get up and head into the kitchen to get a drink. The movie emotions are still swirling in my chest, I don't want to move on so soon.

Rally follows me. "Hey, are you okay?"

"Oh yeah," I laugh it off but I know he can tell I've been crying. My eyelids always turn red, I don't even try to lie about it. "I just love that movie. It feels wrong to move onto something else so quickly."

He wraps his arms around me and pulls me against his chest. I'm a little surprised but it feels good. He's warm. Cozy, even. And I can tell he works out. When he pulls back I smile awkwardly. I have no idea what to say. I scan the room and then look at my glass on the counter.

"I'm sorry, was that too forward?" Rally shoves his hands in his pockets. He seems nervous. "I think you're really great and I... uh... you just seemed like you could use a hug."

"It was fine. I mean, I liked it. I mean, thanks." I better change the subject here quick. "So have you been rooming with these guys for long?"

"The roommates come and go but I've been here for a few years. This is my house—I own it and they rent from me. I didn't like living here alone and so I opened it up to guys from church. They're slobs but I'm kind of like their mom and make them pick up after themselves. It works out pretty well. I mean, I'd much rather be sharing this house with a real mom, I mean my kid's mom, I mean..."

He's rambling and making a disaster of this conversation but it's cute. He runs his hand through his hair, tousling it into an irresistible mess. "Boy, is it hot in here?"

I laugh out loud and we keep talking. I feel my shoulders relax and I lean against the counter. Soon I find my gaze drifting to his mouth. I'm not even listening to what he's saying.

Focus, Julianne. *You have plans. Two weeks. Dream school. East Coast.*

I look again from the warmth of his eyes to his lips. *Stop it.*

But then my eyes go even further rogue and slide to his chest. His firm, muscular chest that I'd just been pressed against.

I take a step towards him. *What am I doing?* He's still talking but I'm not really listening.

I see his wavy hair, standing up where he'd run his hands through it. I wonder what it would feel like to run my hands through it.

I take another step closer. My mind screams at me. *Seriously, what are you doing?? You are leaving to fulfill your dreams in two weeks.* But I can't pull my eyes away from his lips.

He stops talking. Mid-sentence, I think. I smell his aftershave and feel the warmth of his skin. There's stubble along his jawline. I meet his eyes and see a question there. Then, I kiss him.

Chapter 4

"You kissed him??" Adelynn's eyes are popping out of her head. All three nieces are lying on their tummies looking down at me from my bed. When I snuck in last night they were all asleep and there was no room for me so I got the trundle. My face is a mirror of Adelynn's. Yup. I kissed him. *What was I thinking?*

Shela rolls over onto her back and flings her arms open, sending her stuffed bunny flying. "An' then the birds singed!"

"Is this true love or something?" Savvy rolls her eyes but she's soaking up this story every bit as much as Adelynn and Shela.

"So what happened next?" Adelynn probes.

"Well," I wince a little, "my friend came in and told me it was time to go."

"Did she see you kissing??" Her face. She couldn't be more serious. I bite my lips to keep from laughing.

But did McKell see us? "I don't think so. But I think she knew something was up because it was snowing awkwardness on the ride home."

"When do you see him next?" Adelynn can hardly stand not knowing everything. I can see it in her eyes. It's like she's watching a scary movie, like Frozen when you don't know if Ana's going to make it yet.

"I don't know if I'm going to see him again. I was planning on spending every minute of Christmas with you girls."

Adelynn is outraged but it's Savvy who speaks up first.

"Wait, you kissed him and you don't even know if you're going to see him again?" She sits back against the wall and crosses her arms. "This isn't Cinderella."

"Yeah," Shela cries, "you can't kiss and run, those are the rules!" I wonder where she learned those rules.

"Auntie Juju, you've got to see him again!" Adelynn looks like the oven timer is going off and she can't find a grown up to take the cookies out before they burn. If I don't see Rally again, I'm going to burn the cookies! I just can't disappoint her. I thought spending Christmas with my nieces would make it the best but it looks like they won't be satisfied unless I reenact a Hallmark movie. I do like Hallmark movies...

"There is an ice skating activity tonight... And it doesn't start until late so I guess I could spend the whole day with you and still go."

The girls jump up and down on my bed and cheer.

When I get to the ice rink I freeze up. I can't go in. I can't see him again.

I drop my head onto the steering wheel. Even if I was interested in him, which I'm not because I'm leaving for my dream school in two weeks, this would not be the way to start a relationship. He probably thinks I'm such a floozy!

Why did I kiss him?? I must have gotten caught up in the moment. It was all that lovey-dovey talk with my nieces. They broke my focus. Or maybe it was because McKell had been trashing on him all night and all I could see was this adorably attractive man. Did I kiss him to spite McKell? No, I thought he was cute and I enjoyed talking with him. But I'm not usually one to move so fast. I mean he was practically mid-sentence when I slobbered on him.

I pull out my phone to text McKell that I'm not coming when a knock sounds on my window and I jump. Rally is crouching outside smiling at me. Oh gosh, here we go. Watch me die. I roll down my window.

"Are you skating?" He has skates slung over his shoulder like he plays hockey in his free time. I start to feel really warm. *What is wrong with me?*

"You know," I squeak, "I don't think I will after all."

But he's opening my door and pulling me out. And he doesn't let go of my hand. "C'mon," he tugs me gently. "I'll help you."

We walk to the skate rental and I'm whipping my head around looking for McKell. Is she here? Does she see him holding my hand? Does everyone see me holding his hand? I try to be cool but I'm a mess.

"What size?" he asks me.

I feel the blood drain from my face. Is he asking me my ring size? I can't speak.

He looks a little confused and repeats himself, "What size skates?"

I laugh nervously. Right. "Uh, seven and a half."

I grab my skates and head for the bench. He sits down beside me and starts tying his skates. I don't put mine on. I just lean back against the wall and breathe. Heavily.

"Hey, are you okay?" he looks up at me while he wraps the laces around his ankle.

I have to tell him. I have to tell him that I'm leaving in two weeks so nothing can happen between us. My nieces are going to be so disappointed. I take a big breath and let it all out.

"We need to talk about last night. I shouldn't have kissed you. I don't know what I was thinking."

But before I can finish he says, "I know what you were thinking." He double knots the laces on his second skate and turns to grin at me. "You were thinking that you've never met anyone so handsome."

I laugh and feel the tension leave my shoulders. "I mean it. I hardly know you and it was wrong of me to give you a message that was misleading."

He kneels down in front of me and starts tying my skates. "I don't think you misled me at all. I think you told me exactly how you were feeling."

I feel like I've lost control of this conversation.

I have to tell him. I have to tell him I have plans. I have plans and I feel like they are slipping further away. I look around. Where is McKell when I need her? I try to think of what she would say if she were here. *He's old and gross,* I tell myself. But my heart puts up a fight. He's not gross. He smells amazing, like he showered and put on deodorant right before coming here. I chance a look at his forearms as he ties my skates. Worked out, then showered and put on deodorant. *Dang it.* I remind myself that I should be telling him that I'm leaving in two weeks instead of checking him out again. I'm still scolding myself when he grabs my hand and pulls me off the bench.

"Now let's skate."

When I get home that night it's pretty late but the light in the kitchen is still on. I tiptoe in and see my mom reading at the counter with a steaming mug.

"You still up?" I ask her.

"Of course," she smiles. I'm an adult who's lived away from home for four years and she still waits up for me. My throat feels thick. It's nice to come home to someone.

I sit on a stool next to her and she grabs the kettle and pours some hot water into an empty mug that she has waiting. "Tea or chocolate?" she asks.

Normally I'd go for a peppermint herbal tea but tonight? "Chocolate."

Mom raises an eyebrow and pours in a packet of hot chocolate mix. She sets it in front of me and takes her stool.

"Did you have fun tonight?"

I feel like she knows more than she's letting on. I squint my eyes at her and stir my drink. "Yes."

"Who did you skate with?"

She totally knows. "Just a guy I met." I sip slowly and lick the foam from my lips.

"You know," she's totally giving herself away now, "you can always get a job here in town, live at home, get your degree online."

"You were totally there!" I laugh. "Were you spying on me? Who told you?"

She sets her mug down and laughs with me. "Bishop might have called to say they'd run out of cups and that his wife could go get more but that I might want an excuse to stop by the rink and see who you'd been skating with all night."

Did I skate with Rally the whole night? I guess I did. It didn't feel like that long. He was so easy to be with. And he made me laugh.

"So who is he?"

"He's just a guy, Mom." An incredibly charming and attractive one. "Besides, I've got plans. Plans that I'm excited about."

"You know what they say: Life is what happens while you're making plans."

"Just because I skated with him around the rink a couple times does not mean we are getting married."

"Well, honey, it doesn't mean you didn't enjoy his company either. Sometimes you make plans for yourself and then the Lord makes different plans for you. Sometimes His plans are way better."

"Are you finally admitting that I was an accident?"

She shakes her head and smiles. "You were not an accident."

"Not an accident to the Lord, you mean, but a... *pleasant surprise* for you and Dad."

"If anyone had asked me when Nora was born if I thought I'd have another baby in eight years, I'd have told you that you were crazy. I was almost 40 when you finally joined the family. But no, you were very planned. I felt inspired to follow the Lord's plan instead of my own."

She doesn't have to say the rest. I know what she means.

"When do you see him next?"

"I don't know. I was planning on spending Christmas with my family before I move across the country, not wooing some guy." I dunk the marshmallows with my spoon and watch them slowly disintegrate.

"Well, what's the next activity?"

"I guess everyone is going skiing tomorrow but it's not really my jam. And that's prime family time."

The next day I wake up to this horrible smell. And just like that, I am off to the slopes as fast as my little heinie will carry me. I'm dedicated to my *awesome auntie* status but barf is where I draw the line.

Chapter 5

"Skis or board?" The kid behind the rental counter is scruffy. Like he only shaves when he sees his mom. And he doesn't see her often.

I bite my lip and look around. Rally is standing by the door holding a snowboard. He looks like he's up here every weekend.

I don't ski or snowboard so, why not? "Give me a board."

We ride the lift up to the top of the hill. It's a long way down. I start to feel nervous. It keeps going up and up and I keep thinking how am I going to get down this thing?

Then the ski lift stops mid-mountain and we are just swinging there. This is the perfect time to tell him. Just tell him you're leaving and you'd love to be friends. *Or you can get a job in town, live at home, get your degree online and see what happens.*

"Is Rally short for anything?"

"Ya, it's short for Ralph. But no one ever calls me Ralph, not even my family."

McKell was right! Ralph is not the most handsome name. I definitely prefer Rally.

It's like he can read my thoughts because next he says, "When my mom was pregnant with me she was doing some family history work and found the name of a relative who died on the battlefield in France during the First World War. She thought it was so tragic, him dying there all alone with no family, that she decided to name me after him. You know, let him know that he wasn't forgotten."

It's such a sweet story. And it makes the name not so bad.

"My mom loves family history stuff. Every year she tells us the same story about my great-grandfather during the Depression. He took a teaching job up in northern Canada to pay the bills. He was so lonely at Christmas that he traveled for three days just so he could be with his family for 24 hours."

When we get to the top of the mountain I start to feel light-headed. I look back down the way we came. It's like we are on the edge of a cliff.

"If we go this way we can take the blue run and then hit this black diamond," Rally points to the map of trails.

My head is swimming with blues and blacks. I search desperately for some green.

"How about this one?" I point weakly at the only green run I see on the board.

Rally hesitates. "You know how to snowboard, right?"

I laugh weakly, "Not exactly."

"How many times have you been?"

I stop laughing and wince. "This would be my first."

He lets out a long breath and stares down the mountain as though he too has just realized how high up we are. Then he looks back at me and grabs my shoulders. "You've got this, Julianne. We'll do it together."

We take the green run and he shows me how to keep my weight back on my heels so I don't catch my front lip. I try it out and catch my front lip anyway. Falling downhill onto your face is no joke. I try again and this time I make it a little further before I fall on my face.

He zigzags down the hill in front of me then he stops and waits. "Try to fall on your butt!" he calls up to me. "It's a lot softer!"

Haha, I think to myself. I haul my big, soft butt up and try again. Midway down the hill I'm so tired and sore I can hardly move. When I fall I just lie there. I can't do it. My wrists hurt so bad and now my bum is hurting too. My face feels raw from the many ice exfoliations.

I stare up at the clear sky above me, wishing I were back at home curled up in my chair reading a book. With a blazing fire and some hot chocolate.

And cookies. It sounds so nice. Then Rally's face appears above me and I know I'm not going to be staying in this position for long.

"You've got to get down the hill. You can't give up."

I pull off my gloves and swipe at my nose. "Rally, I can't do it. I'm exhausted and I can only go a few feet before I wipe out. You go on without me. I'll just lay here until the ski patrol comes by and picks me up."

He doesn't budge. I can see he's not going to let me off easy.

"Or better yet," I try again, "when you get to the bottom you send the ski patrol up to rescue me."

"Julianne." He looks into my eyes and I get all warm and tingly. "I am not giving up on you. I will wait for you as long as it takes."

I know we're talking about skiing here but my insides melt and I get this gooey, dreamy look on my face.

He cracks a grin like he knows exactly what I'm thinking and then pulls me up. No mercy. So romantic.

That night when I get home, Mom is reading a story to all the grandkids. The fire is crackling and they are all wrapped up on the couch in blankets. Adelynn waves to me. She's still a bit pale. Her hair is slicked into a damp braid like she's just had a bath. Shela's already asleep, drooling on the arm of the couch. There's hot chocolate and cookies on the counter. I collapse onto a stool and start shoveling cookies like I haven't seen food in a week.

"There's soup in the fridge," Mom calls to me as she pulls out another book. She's a master storyteller and she has each of the grandkids completely mesmerized. I think the story will be the one about my great-grandfather coming home for Christmas during the Depression but it's not. It's one I haven't heard before.

It is about my great-grandfather but it's about ten years later when he met my great-grandmother during World War II. Clive and Dorothy. They met at a serviceman's ball and it was love at first sight. Well, it was for him at least. Mom's voice is soothing as she reads.

"*Dorothy*, he'd whispered in her ear as they swayed to the music, *I know I'm a fool for saying this but dancing here with you, I feel as though I'm on my farm again, standing on the back forty,* he laughed softly and pulled her closer. *I'll be darned if I can't see the Manitoba prairie stretching for miles in your eyes.*"

All the grandkids laugh when Mom reads that. But those words sink deep into my heart. I stir my soup distractedly as she reads on.

"A silly thing to say– that he saw the prairie in her eyes. Perhaps it was simply because her eyes were the color of a rich soil ready for planting. But Dorothy had felt her heart swell at those words. What he had described was his home. He saw his home in her eyes. She was a practical girl but she couldn't think of anything more romantic."

Chapter 6

The next day I am so sore. My bum, my wrists, my thighs, muscles I didn't even know I had... Everything. I lay on the couch and watch back-to-back princess movies with my sick nieces. I glance at my phone on the armrest and tap its blank screen. I wonder what Rally's doing. If he had as much fun as I did yesterday. Then I wonder about McKell. She didn't come skiing. And she didn't answer the text I sent her.

My phone pings. I reach for it like it's the last cinnamon roll on Christmas morning.

Rally: Are you coming tonight?

"What Auntie Juju? Who is it?" Shela snatches the phone from my hands. She looks at it for a few seconds and then hands it back. "I can't read," she shrugs.

I grab my phone and text back. There's a flurry of excitement in my chest.

Julianne: Depends on the activity. I can hardly move so anything away from my couch is out.

Rally: How about I come to you then?

Do I want to introduce my family to my not-quite boyfriend? That's what this feels like. Like he's my boyfriend, only we haven't made it official yet. The flurry in my chest freezes. Is that what this is? I do like him. A lot. And I feel great when I'm with him. I feel like... how would I describe it? It's definitely nothing I've felt for anyone else before. I try not to think about what this means for my plans.

Julianne: Sure. My family is playing games tonight. It's a Christmas tradition to play the one my brother made up. It's super dorky but so much fun.

Rally: Sounds like a blast. I'm in.

I haul myself off the couch and head to my room to get cleaned up—I should shower and brush my teeth at the very least. Maybe a little mascara and lip gloss. Nothing too fancy. He'd know something was up if I claimed that I watched princess movies on the couch all day in full makeup and curled hair.

When he arrives, Mom is a bustle of nervous energy. She's tidying and throwing together some last minute fudge and telling everyone to act natural.

"Mom, relax," I pick a pillow up off the floor and toss it on the couch. "Rally's really nice. He won't care if there are toys on the floor."

"I know he's nice," she says as she frantically puts toys in a basket. "That's exactly why I want to make a good impression!"

I roll my eyes but jump and run to the door when the bell rings.

"Hey." I try to be real cool. He looks amazing in a down puffer and jeans.

"Hey," he grins. I hear some giggles and see my nieces peeking their heads around the corner to get a look at Rally.

"Julianne's older siblings are just getting kids to bed and we can't play the game without them," Mom calls from the kitchen as she cuts the fudge. "Do you mind if we play some other games while we wait for them? We haven't been able to play this great couples game yet with Julianne and I'd love to pull it out and teach you."

My eyes dart to Rally to see if he's okay with this 'couple' reference. *Sorry,* I mouth. But he cracks this killer smile and I just can't believe he's still on the market and standing on my doorstep.

Mom smiles over her shoulder as she climbs the stairs to the loft to retrieve the cards. I can tell she already loves him. Heck, I just love him. I try to quell the dreamy look in my eyes but she's totally onto me.

Just then my sister Nora walks into the room rubbing her hands together. "Alright losers, get ready to– Rally?"

Rally looks surprised but he recovers quickly. "Nora? Long time no see!" He pulls my sister into a big slappy man hug.

"What's it been, ten years since we were at college together?"

"Oh gosh, you're making me feel old now."

Then she gestures over her shoulder. "I want you to meet my husband. He's getting our kids to bed but he'll be out soon. What about you? You probably have six kids, am I right?"

Rally kind of scratches his head as he searches for what to say. "Still looking for the right one, actually."

"No kidding. We all thought you'd be the first one off the market." Nora looks between me and Rally. I get this sinking feeling in my gut.

"So, what are you doing here?" Nora asks, though I think she has her suspicions.

Rally shoves his hands in his pockets. He looks uncomfortable.

"Rally and I met at one of the singles activities," I jump in. "I invited him over to play games with us tonight."

Nora's eyebrows shoot up. She doesn't look so chummy now. She looks like she's siding with McKell. "You're dating my baby sister?"

Rally looks really uncomfortable now. "Look, we've just been getting to know each other. She's a great girl."

Is that what he thinks of me? A little girl? I cross my arms and tuck my chin like I'm trying to protect my heart. Here I've been thinking we had the beginnings of something special and he thinks I'm a little girl?

Rally looks at his phone. "Hey, I've got to go. Maybe games another time?" He gives me a side hug and waves to Nora. "Good to see you again."

Mom is just coming back downstairs as he closes the door. "I can't believe I found the rules to this game. They are handwritten by your father from before any of you were born."

I glare at Nora and then stalk to my bedroom as Mom says, "Who wants fudge?"

That night I lie on the trundle and watch my nieces' bunny nightlight change colors. Someone is snoring softly but that's not the reason I can't sleep. I'm so mad. It's not Nora's fault but I need someone to blame. I was ready to give up my plans and now I feel like a dummy. A little girl and a dummy.

My door creaks open, the hall light casts a beam over my bed and I see a silhouette enter. Then Nora curls up next to me on my bed. "Are you asleep?"

I don't say anything.

"I'm sorry, Julianne. I didn't mean to ruin your night. I was friends with Rally in college. I haven't seen him in years.

"It was a little weird for me tonight but that's just because I love you so much and I want to protect you. I went all mama bear but I shouldn't have. Rally is a great guy and if you want to date him, you should.

"And if you're worried about his age, don't be. You and I are two peas in a pod and I'm just as old as he is. You've been an old soul since day one. What matters more is how you feel when you're with him.

"I know you're old enough to make your own choices but I hope this helps you feel better about it. Next time he calls, you should say yes."

I squeeze her hand.

But he doesn't call. Christmas passes and New Years arrives and I still don't hear from him.

Chapter 7

Adelynn hands me a black balloon she's just blown up for our family New Years party and I tie it. Savvy is working valiantly on getting a gold balloon inflated bigger than an egg and I'm not sure what Shela's doing but there's a lot of spit involved.

"Did your boyfriend dump you because of Aunt Nora?" Savvy blows into her balloon until her face turns purple. It's still no bigger than a grapefruit.

"He wasn't my boyfriend and he didn't dump me." I take the balloon from her, wipe off the spit and finish it off.

"But you were all smiley and bouncy before and now you're not."

"I'm still smiley." I frown at the balloon as I wrap the end around my fingers and tie it in a knot.

Shela puts her hands on her hips and gives me *the eye*. She learned that from her mom. I've seen my sister give me that eye dozens of times. "You're a sweepy mess, Auntie Juju."

"Alright, I guess I've been a little mopey." I roll my eyes and blow up a silver balloon.

Shela raspberry blows into her balloon. It doesn't inflate even a smidge. She throws it on the table. "And I thought it was true love!"

I smile at her. A small, sad smile. *Me too, kiddo.*

"You should tell him."

"Tell him what?" I flip Savvy's braid.

"That you love him."

Do I? I stretch a balloon out before blowing into it. "It's not that simple."

"Why not?" Shela copies me and pulls the edges of her balloon until they snap back, flinging spit everywhere.

I wipe a drop from my cheek. "Well... what if he doesn't feel the same way about me?"

Shela shakes her head at me as if I'm being silly. "Of course he loves you. He's just afraid of my mom!"

Is he? I mean, does he? Do I even want to know? I think of my plans. My school. My career. Then I think of how I felt when I was with him. For some reason the Manitoba prairie comes to mind. And then I go curl my hair.

The church is already bumping when I arrive. There are tons of cars and people going in with trays of food.

I make my way inside and search for a familiar face. I'm looking for Rally but the person I see first is McKell. I make my way over to her and give her a hug. She hugs me back, so tight. I pull back and see that there are tears in her eyes.

"Kell-Kell? Where have you been?"

"I'm so sorry. I didn't want you to meet Rally because I knew he would just love you. You're my best friend and I didn't want you to go and get married and leave me behind again."

"What do you mean, again?"

"When you went away to university I missed you so much. But it didn't seem like you missed me the same. You were moving on—making new friends, starting a career that would take you other places. I was super sad. And when you didn't get married at school I was happy that you would be coming back here and things would be the same as they always were. But then Rally met you and I could see that he was totally interested in you. I just didn't want to lose you again. But I can see that trying to keep you from living your life is losing you in a worse way..."

"McKell, you are my best friend. I need our friendship. No matter where life takes me, I will always need you. Besides, I just met Rally. I'm nowhere near getting married."

I hug her and we spend the rest of the night together dancing, playing Minute-To-Win-It games and eating so many cookies.

Soon everyone is gathering for the countdown and making sure they are standing next to the person they are hoping to kiss when the clock strikes twelve. Everyone starts screaming, "Ten! Nine! Eight!"

And then I see him. Rally is looking right at me from across the gym and he's not counting with everyone else. He hands his cup to some random person and makes his way directly to me. He pushes through the crowd and reaches me just as everyone screams, *Happy New Year!*

There's confetti flying and streamers and noise makers buzzing. It's deafening. He tries to say something but I can't hear him. I squint and cup my ear. He tries again but I still can't hear him. I shake my head and mouth, *I can't hear you.*

He looks at me for what feels like a long time, like he's trying to decide something. Then he takes my face in both his hands and he kisses me. It's soft and sweet. It feels like a steaming mug of hot chocolate, being wrapped up in a blanket, sinking into my favorite chair after a long day, snuggling in front of a fire.

He pulls back and searches my face for a reaction. I want to tell him all about Clive and Dorothy and the Manitoba prairie. I want to tell him that I finally know why I kissed him in the first place. I want to tell him that being with him feels like coming home for Christmas, but I can't. There's still too much noise. And so, I kiss him back.

AUTHOR BIOGRAPHIES

Victoria Colver

Victoria Colver grew up across the street from a bus stop with a direct line to the public library. Coming home with many Enid Blyton adventures and Nancy Drew mysteries, her parents read to her every night. She now enjoys reading clean and uplifting words in many genres, especially snuggled up with her kids. She crafts stories sparked by her family history and hopes to inspire others to explore their own genealogy. This is her first publication. You can find her at facebook/VictoriaColver.

Clark Graham

Clark Graham is a longtime member of Science Fiction and Fantasy Writers of America. He has written over fifty books in multiple genres and is working on more. He retired from his day job so he could write full time at his North Idaho home. You can reach him at elvenshore@gmail.com.

Deb Graham

Pacific Northwest author Deb Graham is the author of over 30 books, including cozy mysteries, paranormal, historical fiction, cookbooks, and women's fiction, plus the best-selling Cruise Addict's Wife series. All of her books are clean and wholesome and even the crime novels leave readers feeling upbeat at the end. Deb's goal is to "push back the darkness" in the world through her writing. Her interests include her family and traveling anywhere that requires a suitcase, or better yet, a passport. Deb lives with her author husband and although many mystery writers say they love their spouse and have several beloved cats, Deb does love the man but, sadly, has no cats. Find her at: http://www.debgrahamauthor.com/

L.P. Masters

Born and raised in the cloudy streets of the Seattle area, L.P. Masters spent her fair share of time staring out rain-streaked windows and writing books in her free time. Masters has always had extremely vivid dreams, which often spark inspiration for her novels. These days she lives on the less-drizzly side of the state, but she doesn't have as much free time, or as much sleep as she used to, since she is currently raising a handful of rambunctious kids. But she still manages to write her dream-inspired science fiction books. Visit her website at www.lpmasters.com, or connect with her at https://facebook.com/lpmastersauthor

Shanna L. K. Miller

Shanna L. K. Miller's passion for literature was piqued while reading Arthurian tales in her parents closet. She published her first piece while in sixth grade. Her Poet's Nook among pine trees at her grandmother's cabin was a favorite hideaway. Miller's poetry took an angsty, introspective turn during high school and young adulthood. Now she writes whatever strikes her fancy. An eclectic reader, Shanna consumes books and chocolate with equal alacrity.

Shanna's interests include spending time with her husband, children and grandchildren. She relishes travel, climbing pyramids and lighthouses and helping her husband with their YouTube channel @global_birding. Connecting with family, friends and water fitness fuel her creative energy. Shanna sees possibilities. Contact Shanna on Instagram at shannalkmiller. Find her on Facebook at Shanna L. K. Miller Poet/Storyteller.

Tyler Scott Powell

Tyler Scott Powell enjoys long conversations and short stories. He has found a great deal of direction for his own life in the Hero's Journey story structure and hopes to be able to help young adults slay life's dragons.

Alli Riggs

Alli is an author of more than 25 books. She loves binge-reading over binge-watching, anything that makes her laugh, and creating fantastical worlds she and her readers can get lost in. She lives with her family in Eastern Washington. If you'd like to be on her mailing list, go to JANAE LCO.com to sign-up.

Kathryn Rosenbaum

Kathryn and her husband live in Washington State, surrounded by evergreens and apple trees. And lilacs, but the lilacs make her sneeze. She is most at-home with teenagers, and among her other quirks, she likes black licorice and doesn't care for chocolate. Please don't hate her. Kathryn's superpowers include winning card games, killing house plants, and remembering where her kids left their shoes.

https://www.amazon.com/stores/author/B0CTK7RK2V?

Kim Roth

As a stay-at-home mom for twenty-five years, Kim has been too preoccupied finding Lego pieces, reading bedtime stories, cheering at sporting events, and editing her high school kids' essays to do much of her own writing. Having developed the organization and disaster-management skills necessary to run a household of seven, she now finds herself in forced retirement from full-time motherhood as the kids leave home to begin thriving as adults and is finally beginning to write the stories life has given her.

Kim has a bachelor's degree in English–which her kids tease helped her become fluent in her native language–and teaches the violin. She and her husband live in the Inland Northwest, have five children and two grandchildren, and love to waterski, snow-ski, hike and travel.

Made in United States
Troutdale, OR
10/27/2024

24135679R00159